1994

*Capitalism, Socialism,
and Democracy
Revisited*

A Journal of Democracy Book

Capitalism, Socialism, and Democracy Revisited

Edited by Larry Diamond
and Marc F. Plattner

The Johns Hopkins University Press
Baltimore and London

Chapter 13 originally appeared in the *Journal of Democracy,* April 1993. The remainder of this volume appeared in a special issue of the *Journal of Democracy,* July 1992.

The Johns Hopkins University Press
2715 North Charles Street
Baltimore, Maryland 21218-4319
The Johns Hopkins Press Ltd., London

Library of Congress Cataloging-in-Publication Data
Capitalism, socialism, and democracy revisited / edited by Larry Diamond and Marc F. Plattner.
    p.   cm. — (A Journal of democracy book)
    "Chapter 13 originally appeared in the Journal of democracy, April 1993. The remainder of this volume appeared in a special issue of the Journal of democracy, July 1992"—Verso t.p.
    Includes bibliographical references and index.
    ISBN 0-8018-4746-X (alk. paper). —ISBN 0-8018-4747-8 (pbk. : alk. paper)
    1. Democracy. 2. Capitalism. 3. Socialism. 4. Comparative government. 5. Comparative economics.   I. Diamond, Larry Jay.   II. Plattner, Marc F., 1945–   .   III. Journal of democracy. July 1992 and April 1993.   IV. Series.
JC421.C24   1993
320.3—dc20   93-4362

A catalog record for this book is available from the British Library.

CONTENTS

ACKNOWLEDGMENTS

As is explained in the Introduction that follows, this volume is the culmination of a project undertaken by the *Journal of Democracy*. Its previous stages comprised the convening of an international symposium in Washington, D.C., on 3 April 1992, and the publication in July 1992 of a special issue of the *Journal of Democracy* based on the symposium presentations. Finally, an essay by Seymour Martin Lipset (first published in the April 1993 issue of the *Journal of Democracy*) was specially prepared to serve as a conclusion to this volume.

The entire project was supported by a generous grant from The Pew Charitable Trusts of Philadelphia, Pennsylvania. Kevin Quigley and his colleagues at Pew helped to shape the format of this project and provided extremely useful advice and encouragement throughout. We are enormously grateful to them for their assistance. We also wish to thank the Lynde and Harry Bradley Foundation and the Smith Richardson Foundation for their continuing support of the Journal.

In the course of seeking out authors for this project, we consulted widely among the *Journal*'s Editorial Board; as always, they proved to be an excellent source of advice. We also want to express special thanks to the four Board members who served as moderators of the sessions at the April 1992 symposium—Ernest J. Wilson III, Juan J. Linz, Atul Kohli, and Seymour Martin Lipset.

The *Journal* staff performed with its customary distinction in helping us to carry out this project. Phil Costopoulos did a superb job of editing the manuscripts, and Debbie Liang and Kathy Vitz played a key role not only in the editorial process but in making the necessary organizational arrangements for the symposium. Patricia Loo and Kurt Oeler, who joined the staff later in the project, contributed greatly to preparing this volume for publication, and Kurt did a fine job of compiling the index.

We are also grateful for the assistance provided by our friends at the Johns Hopkins University Press—Henry Tom and his colleagues in the book division and Marie Hansen, Carol Hamblen, and their colleagues in the journals division.

The *Journal*'s parent organization, the National Endowment for Democracy, has supported us in this as in all our other endeavors. The Endowment's president, Carl Gershman, opened the symposium with some well-chosen words, and Margaret Ferry, Megan Connor, and other Endowment staff members provided invaluable assistance in arranging both the symposium and a reception in honor of Seymour Martin Lipset that immediately followed it.

Finally, we wish to thank our authors, many of whom travelled great distances to participate in the symposium, and all of whom did a splendid job of writing and revising their essays. It has been a pleasure working with them to produce a volume that we believe offers the most comprehensive and penetrating contemporary analysis of the relationship among capitalism, socialism, and democracy. We hope that our readers will concur in this assessment, and that they will find this book a fitting tribute to the extraordinary work on this subject that Joseph Schumpeter produced half a century ago.

INTRODUCTION

Larry Diamond and Marc F. Plattner

Over 50 years ago, in 1942, Joseph Schumpeter published the first edition of *Capitalism, Socialism and Democracy*, his classic study of the relationship between political democracy and alternative economic systems. It is a book of magisterial scope and great insight that continues to be widely read and cited by social scientists today. Yet many of its central conclusions have been called sharply into question by the developments of recent years. It thus provides an ideal starting point for reflection about a question that is no less important or pressing today.

Though an admirer of capitalism's achievements and not an advocate of socialism, Schumpeter sought to show that "a socialist form of society will inevitably emerge from an equally inevitable decomposition of capitalist society." While his own analysis was complex and highly original, Schumpeter noted that this conclusion was "rapidly becoming the general opinion, even among conservatives." He also argued that, in principle if not necessarily in practice, there is no incompatibility between socialism and political democracy.

Half a century later, the general opinion on these matters appears to have undergone a wholesale transformation. Socialism as Schumpeter defined it—"an institutional pattern in which control over the means of production and over production itself is vested with a central authority" and "in which, as a matter of principle, the economic affairs of society belong to the public and not the private sphere"—is clearly in ideological retreat and political disarray.

For most of the past decade, the United States and other key countries in the West have been governed by conservative, pro-private enterprise parties. The democratic socialist parties of Western Europe have rediscovered the virtues of markets and entrepreneurship. In what used to be called the Third World, state-controlled economies have stagnated, and structural adjustment and privatization have become the order of the day. Finally, and most dramatically, communism has collapsed both in Eastern Europe and the former Soviet Union. Moreover, there seems to be widespread agreement—especially in the postcommunist countries—that democracy cannot succeed without the introduction of a market economy.

Even before the demise of the Soviet Union, its communist rulers had acknowledged the failure of centralized planning and adopted the goal of moving toward a market economy. This about-face on the part of the Soviet leadership made possible the approval of some striking documents on economic matters by the Conference on Security and Cooperation in Europe (CSCE), whose membership embraced the Soviet Union and its former East European satellites as well as the countries of Western Europe, the United States, and Canada. These documents may perhaps be regarded as an official statement of the opinion that now generally prevails on the issues of the economy and democracy.

On 11 April 1990, the Bonn Conference on Economic Cooperation in Europe affirmed that "democratic institutions and economic freedom foster economic and social progress"; that "the performance of market-based economies relies primarily on the freedom of individual enterprise"; and that "economic freedom for the individual includes the right freely to own, buy, sell, and otherwise utilize property." In addition, "recognizing the relationship between political pluralism and market economies," the CSCE members endorsed not only multiparty democracy, the rule of law, and respect for human rights, but "free and competitive market economies where prices are based on supply and demand."

Similarly, the "Charter of Paris for a New Europe," in which the leaders of the CSCE countries on 21 November 1990 officially proclaimed the end of the Cold War, affirmed not only the principles of democracy but the following propositions on the link between politics and economics: "The free will of the individual, exercised in democracy and protected by the rule of law, forms the necessary basis for successful economic and social development. . . . Freedom and political pluralism are necessary elements in our common objective of developing market economies toward sustainable economic growth, prosperity, social justice, expanding employment, and efficient use of economic resources."

The developments and proclamations recounted above might be taken as evidence that capitalism has triumphed over socialism and that there is an essential connection between capitalism and democracy. But there are also grounds on which these conclusions might be challenged. The CSCE documents themselves, for example, speak of "social justice" as well as "economic freedom." Moreover, nowhere do they explicitly mention either capitalism or socialism. This, in turn, raises the question of whether these terms still retain any clear meaning today, and if so how they should be understood. Should Scandinavia's welfare states, for example, be regarded as capitalist, socialist, or something in between? Obviously, the way in which these terms are defined will profoundly affect how one views the degree of linkage or compatibility that exists between either capitalism or socialism and democracy.

This volume is designed to address the full range of questions involved in assessing the relationship between democracy and alternative economic systems. It had its origins in an international symposium convened by the *Journal of Democracy* on 3 April 1992 to commemorate the fiftieth anniversary of the publication of *Capitalism, Socialism and Democracy*. For this symposium we commissioned six papers and six commentaries from some of the world's leading authorities on these questions. Revised and expanded versions of the presentations made at the symposium were subsequently published in a special issue of the *Journal of Democracy* (July 1992), and are now reprinted here.

Each of the six principal authors was asked to contribute an essay setting forth his own view of the relationship between democracy and various economic systems. Each was sent a statement very similar to that which appears above, but also told to feel free to take issue with the way in which we had posed the problem. We encouraged the authors to refer to Schumpeter's original text if they found it pertinent, but did not insist that they do so. While allowing each of them full freedom to determine the focus of his own essay, we also asked that they address themselves to as many as possible of the following specific questions:

• Does political democracy require or depend upon a market economy?

• Does political democracy require private property? If so, how extensive must the sphere of private property be?

• Does political democracy require limitations on the size of the state or on its role in the economy? If so, what is the nature of these limitations?

• How would you define the relationship between democracy and capitalism (as you would define that term)? What specific aspects of capitalism are especially conducive or detrimental to democracy?

• How would you define the relationship between democracy and socialism (as you would define that term)? What specific aspects of socialism are especially conducive or detrimental to democracy?

• Is there a viable "third way" between (or apart from) capitalism and socialism, and if so what are its distinguishing characteristics?

• Are the terms capitalism and socialism still appropriate and useful in discussing the economic requisites of democracy?

• If you believe that democracy requires certain economic arrangements, is this an inherent necessity or might it be overcome with future economic and social progress?

• If you believe that new kinds of economic systems will emerge in the future, to what extent are these likely to be conducive to or compatible with democracy?

The order in which the essays are presented here reflects the structure of the symposium, which was divided into three sessions, each featuring two principal paper givers and two commentators. The latter, who were asked to write briefer essays, were encouraged to put forward their own views as well as their comments on the longer papers presented at their respective sessions. The concluding essay by Seymour Martin Lipset was commissioned especially for this volume.

In selecting the participants for this symposium, we sought to achieve wide diversity both in geographical and professional backgrounds and in political viewpoints. Our authors hail from Asia, Africa, Eastern Europe, and South America, as well as Western Europe and the United States. Their academic disciplines include political science, economics, sociology, and philosophy, and several among them have also played important roles in the public affairs of their own countries. They occupy a wide range of positions on a political spectrum stretching from champions of capitalism to democratic socialists.

This diversity is fully reflected in the very different approaches and viewpoints that inform the essays that follow. Yet taken together, they offer a revealing picture of the state of contemporary thought regarding capitalism, socialism, and democracy. It is fair to say that virtually all the essays show the impact of what Francisco Weffort calls the political "earthquake" of the events of 1989-91. Even those authors who are most sympathetic to socialism endorse a role for the market and stress the value of an independent civil society. At the same time, they are highly critical of free-market enthusiasts (termed neoconservatives by Weffort and neo-liberals by Adam Przeworski) who see unleashing the market as the key to solving all economic and political problems.

Yet even the unabashedly procapitalist authors in this volume tend to acknowledge that the state, to a greater or lesser degree, has a role to play in the economy. All our contributors, then, seem to accept the notion of the mixed economy, though they differ greatly regarding the appropriate mixture between state and market. This may incline some readers to agree with Kyung-won Kim that "striking the right equilibrium has become an essentially technical exercise," but others may find that the degree of ideological passion evident in many of these essays belies that conclusion.

One critical point on which there is a great deal both of passionate disagreement and intellectual uncertainty is the relationship between democracy and economic growth in developing countries. Though there may be a remarkably broad consensus today on the goal of stable and prosperous democracy, there is clearly very little consensus on the means of achieving it.

As the essays in this volume generally reflect, both democracy and market-oriented economies appear to enjoy much brighter prospects today than they did a half-century ago when Schumpeter wrote. Yet their longer-term success is by no means assured. It is our hope that this volume will contribute to a richer debate about how different kinds of economic arrangements can help or hinder the flourishing of democracy.

*Capitalism, Socialism,
and Democracy
Revisited*

1.
THE UNCERTAIN TRIUMPH OF DEMOCRATIC CAPITALISM

Peter L. Berger

Peter L. Berger *is university professor and director of the Institute for the Study of Economic Culture at Boston University. He has previously been professor of sociology at the New School for Social Research, Rutgers University, and Boston College. His numerous books include* The Homeless Mind: Modernization and Consciousness *(with Brigitte Berger and Hansfried Kellner, 1973),* Pyramids of Sacrifice: Political Ethics and Social Change *(1975), and* The Capitalist Revolution *(1986). From 1981 to 1983, he served as U.S. representative to the UN Working Group on the Right to Development.*

In the half-century since it first appeared, Joseph Schumpeter's *Capitalism, Socialism and Democracy* has attained the status of a minor classic, an odd fate given that almost every one of its main propositions has been empirically falsified. I do not know whether the intent behind this symposium is to bury Schumpeter, to praise him, or perhaps to do both. For the most part, I will do none of these, but rather will comment directly on the questions that were posed to the contributors to this volume, questions that can be usefully discussed without particular reference to Schumpeter. Yet I do want to venture one interpretation of this book by an author who, despite his erroneous predictions, continues to be well worth reading. This interpretation, I think, is not without relevance to our present intellectual and political situation.

The interpretation rests upon a simple fact that is often overlooked when Schumpeter's contributions are discussed—namely, that the man was an Austrian to the core, not only by birth but by temperament and world view. His parental home is located in what subsequently became Czechoslovakia, but Schumpeter was born a German-speaking subject of the Habsburg monarchy. That political entity constituted much more than an empire; it comprised a very distinctive civilization whose special character was most strongly manifested by its educated urban classes. A central trait of this civilization was a deep-seated pessimism, frequently verging on melancholia and even masochism. Schumpeter was very much a child of this civilization, notwithstanding the fact that he spent most of his professional life in the United States. The book under consideration here sharply illustrates this pessimism. Schumpeter was anything but a socialist; he would have been delighted to predict that capitalism was the wave of the future. In the book, of course, he predicted the opposite. Capitalism, he thought, would be done in not by its failures, as Marxists believed, but by its very successes (the irony of this view is very Austrian too). The *economic* mechanisms of capitalism would continue to work well, giving rise to social and cultural byproducts that would subvert the capitalist order from within: The "creative destruction" of capitalism (his phrase) would dissolve the moral basis of society, stifle the entrepreneurial spirit, smother the economy in bureaucracy, and bring forth a resentful intelligentsia bent on biting the capitalist hand that feeds it.

To be sure, all of these developments did occur to an extent, but so far capitalism has been eminently successful in surviving them and even in turning them to its own advantage. As to socialism, Schumpeter believed both that it could work economically and that it could be reconciled with democratic forms of government. It is now fairly clear that he was wrong on both counts, at least as the empirical record so far indicates.

I suppose that one could apply the term "cognitive masochism" to an intellectual posture that defines integrity as predicting that course of events which one least desires. (It is no accident that the Baron von Sacher-Masoch, whose name simultaneously evokes one of the world's most delicious pastries and one of its most complicated neuroses, was also an Austrian.) This posture is well exemplified by an episode in Schumpeter's early career. Just after World War I, he was invited to join the commission planning the nationalization of industries in Germany. A friend asked him how he could have accepted this invitation, since as an economist he was strongly opposed to nationalization. He replied: "If a person wants to commit suicide, it is good to have a physician in attendance." While there is surely a certain grandeur in such an attitude—a stoic fortitude that looks without flinching at the world as it is and not as one would like it to be—we should also remember that no special epistemological privilege attaches to pessimism.

Still, Schumpeter's attitude can serve as a useful corrective to the current mood, which is one of triumphalism as far as capitalism and democracy are concerned. It is not only the Soviet empire that has collapsed, but, or so it seems, all the ideas that legitimated socialism elsewhere. The left, or so it seems, has bitten the dust. Ahead lies an age of victorious democratic capitalism, an American century, perhaps even "the end of history." It seems to me that this triumphalism is a bit premature and that a dose of Schumpeterian pessimism would be rather salutary. Be this as it may, my own approach to the issues at hand is neither masochistic nor triumphalist.

Democracy and the Market

Does political democracy require or depend upon a market economy? Here is one question where caution is *not* called for: the answer is a resounding *yes*. The reason for it is strictly empirical: the evidence overwhelmingly suggests it. That evidence makes possible three simple but far-reaching propositions: 1) There has been no case of political democracy that has *not* been a market economy. (Or, if one prefers a sharper formulation, there has been no case of democratic socialism.) 2) There have been numerous cases of *non*democratic market economies. 3) When market economies are successful over a period of time, pressure for democratization inevitably ensues.

A little farther on I will consider some possible explanations of these empirical findings, but first it is necessary to clarify the meaning of some key terms. It seems to me that one most usefully discusses capitalism and socialism if one understands them quite narrowly as two alternative modern systems of production (as, indeed, the Marxists have always done)—the one based on market forces and private ownership of at least (a handy Marxist term) the "commanding heights" of the economy, the other based on state control and on public ownership of these "commanding heights." By these definitions, an oft-cited "socialist" country like Sweden (even in the heyday of Social Democratic governance) is, I would contend, no such thing. The confusion here is between production and distribution. Sweden, like most of the other Northern European democracies, has developed a very generous welfare state—that is, a very elaborate system of distribution and redistribution. But the welfare state, even in its Scandinavian apotheosis, continues to rest on a capitalist system of production; indeed, only the affluence created by the latter makes this welfare state possible. Sweden is not, as its proponents keep saying, a "third way"; rather, it is a variation on the "first way." Indeed, under modern conditions, there is no "third way," but only an array of variations on the two alternative models.

Does political democracy require private property? If so, how much of it? The answer to the first question is almost certainly yes. The answer to the second question is that no one knows for sure.

The question here really is whether there can be a market economy without private property; the question of whether political democracy requires a market economy has already been answered in the affirmative. Put differently, the question is whether there could be such a thing as "market socialism"—the important enterprises remaining in public ownership but competing with one another under market forces. Such a system can be imagined in theory. The Polish economist Oskar Lange first drew up a formal model of market socialism way back in the 1930s and similar work has been done in more recent times. Two countries, Yugoslavia and Hungary, ran experiments with "market socialism" for some 30 years each. Both these experiments, it can now be said with certainty, failed.

How can one explain this failure? Both entrepreneurial risk-taking and financial controls over these risks (say, a businessman starting an enterprise and the banker loaning him the capital to do so) depend on the motives of private owners, less because of the joys of ownership as such than because of the control that ownership bestows when it is legally secure. The manager of a socialist enterprise who is told by the economic command centers, which own his firm and in a real sense own *him* (for, outside the command structure, there are no worthwhile jobs), to go out and act as an entrepreneur is in fact told to do the impossible or at least the highly improbable—to *simulate* capitalist entrepreneurship. In practice, it seems, this simply does not work. What does work, up to a point, is opening up sectors of a socialist economy to private enterprise. This occurred in both Yugoslavia and Hungary, and it has been happening quite successfully in China, both before and since the repression of June 1989. What also happens in such cases, though, is that the capitalist sector develops a dynamism that will increasingly threaten the much less productive socialist sector—a development that is probably giving the Beijing gerontocracy some sleepless nights.

Political democracy requires a market economy, and a market economy requires private property. But how much of it? In other words, what segments of the economy may be held in public ownership before the basis of democracy is threatened? There must be some limit beyond which state ownership begins to threaten democracy. Yet present knowledge does not permit us to discern exactly where this limit is. Comparisons between existing capitalist democracies (say, between countries like Austria and Switzerland, which have quite different levels of public ownership) suggest that there is a good deal of leeway. The libertarian view that each step in the direction of public ownership is a step toward despotism is not borne out by the evidence. On the other hand, given the empirical linkage between democracy and capitalism, policy makers would be well-advised to be cautious in expanding public ownership.

This leads logically to the more general question concerning what limits on state authority over the economy are needed if democracy is to continue. Clearly, democracy cannot coexist with an all-powerful state. Again, one could talk at length about definitions, but the commonsensical definition of democracy (shared, incidentally, by most political scientists) will serve adequately here. This defines democracy in terms of two institutions—regular (and real) elections, and a body of (real) civil rights and liberties. Both institutions serve to limit state power. To put the case in elegant philosophical terms, the first institution makes sure that periodically the bastards can be thrown out of office, while the other makes sure that there are some things the bastards cannot do even when they hold office.

Yet when it comes to the question of limiting the role of the state *in the economy*, we are back, I think, to the aforementioned insight that there must be a threshold somewhere, but that we are not sure just where it is. We do know the extremes. Socialism, the maximal role of the state in the economy, makes democracy impossible and wrecks the economy to boot. At the other pole, at least under modern conditions, a minimalist, *laissez-faire* sort of state is empirically impossible, and there is no such case. (Some readers may think of Hong Kong. It is no such thing, but rather a very efficient, if thoroughly undemocratic, conspiracy of Chinese businessmen and British civil servants.) In between, once more, there seems to be a good deal of leeway—say, between the United States, a *relatively* modest case of state intervention, and much more statist cases like Japan or even France. All are market economies, all are democracies. It is important to focus not so much on the *degree* of state intervention as on the *nature* of that intervention. Does state intervention in the economy move *with* market forces or *against* them? Thus, arguably, the Japanese state intervenes in the economy without undermining the dynamics of the market; by contrast, the argument has been made that the growing ranks of EC Eurocrats (carriers of the "Brussels syndrome") will do serious damage if left unchecked.

An Asymmetrical Relationship

A useful way to describe the relation between democracy and capitalism is to say that it is *asymmetrical*. Capitalism is a necessary—though not sufficient—condition for democracy but democracy is *not* a precondition for capitalism. This, it seems to me, is what the empirical evidence indicates. As it happens, I regret this; I would much prefer a symmetrical relation, where the two institutional arrangements could be seen as the two sides of the same coin of liberty. Alas, they are not. The major contemporary falsifiers of the symmetrical view (the classical libertarian one) are the East Asian cases—notably, the "four little dragons" of South Korea, Taiwan, Hong Kong, and Singapore. All display a vigorous capitalist dynamic, still far from its apex, but in some ways more successful than the Western case. Each one of these post-World War II Asian success stories unfolded under a nondemocratic regime. As for Japan, the greatest of the East Asian success stories, it has been a democracy since losing World War II, but the period when it first established a successful capitalism, the Meiji period (1868-1912), was anything *but* democratic. Two recent capitalist successes, Spain and Chile, both had their takeoffs under dictatorships. Indeed, one might ask

how many Western societies were democratic in our sense at the time
they took off into modern capitalism. Eighteenth-century England, where
it all started, probably was not. The United States, in this as in many
other matters, may be exceptional. Given this evidence, it has been
suggested that democracy is not the regime
best suited to capitalism's birth and early
growth, though it *is* the regime most likely
to emerge after a period of successful
capitalist development.

*"...sustained
and successful
capitalism...opens
up the social space
for civil society,
and as people
become more
affluent they
develop more
ambitious political
aspirations."*

These considerations—to say nothing of
their potentially far-reaching policy
implications—are uncomfortable and full of
uncertainties. More comfortable and more
certain, however, is the reason why
capitalism is necessary for democracy: It
provides the *social space* within which
individuals, groups, and entire institutional
complexes can develop independent of state
control. To use a term that has lately
returned to fashionable usage, capitalism creates space and opportunity
for *civil society*. Conversely, the empirical correlation between socialism
and dictatorship can be explained precisely by the *absence* of such social
space in a socialist system. To achieve this effect, needless to say, it is
not at all important whether the original capitalist class is or is not
inspired by democratic ideas, for it is the consequences of capitalism, *not*
the motives of capitalists, that create the space for democracy. (Adam
Smith, no doubt, would have liked this proposition.) The same
sociological perspective goes a long way toward explaining the
democratizing tendency of sustained and successful capitalism. It opens
up the social space for civil society, and as people become more affluent
they develop more ambitious political aspirations. To put it simply, the
well-fed and well-educated children of poor peasants tend to become
politically uppity, and the same economic system that has made them
well-fed and well-educated provides the space for their new political
aspirations.

Conversely, socialism makes widespread affluence less likely even as
it closes up the social space in which democracy could develop. It is
important to understand that this antidemocratic effect of socialism is
inherently *structural* in origin, and not just the result of some contingent
variety of totalitarian ideology (such as Marxism-Leninism). While
totalitarian ideas—of society as an all-embracing fraternity or of the party
as the infallible embodiment of the force of history—have certainly
served to legitimate socialist dictatorships and to inspire their cadres,
socialism would make democracy highly unlikely even in the absence of
such ideas. The explanation for this is simple: Although there have been

socialist utopias envisaging the control of the economy by independent associations of producers (as in the syndicalist vision), these have remained just that—utopias that are empirically unrealizable except perhaps in small voluntary communities (such as Israeli *kibbutzim* or the communes of nineteenth-century American Shakers) or over short periods of time (as in the workers' and peasants' soviets right after the Bolshevik revolution).

Given the complex nature of a modern or even a modernizing economy, socialism must invariably mean control of the economy *by the state*. In other words, the state is the only "available" control mechanism other than the market. But because of modern technology, the state is *already* a fearsome agglomeration of power. Even the most restrained, democratic state today has more power at its disposal than the most efficient despotisms of premodern times—just imagine Caligula with an empire-wide computer network, Genghis Khan with helicopter gunships, or for that matter Ivan the Terrible with a functioning Internal Revenue Service. To give the modern state direct control over the economy—that is, control of the very livelihood of all or most of its citizens—is to bring about a quantum leap in state power. Such extensive power is difficult if not impossible to reconcile with democracy.

To this explanation, another may be added. Socialism, as Karl Marx well knew, can only be established by a titanic act of expropriation. Yet given the condition of human life in society, individual property will inevitably spring up again (Adam Smith understood *that*). Hence, the socialist expropriation cannot be a one-time-only event, but must be repeated over and over again. Socialism requires eternal vigilance. Such constant expropriation, however, is not feasible in a democratic society, where those who are to be expropriated are free to organize and resist. Dictatorship is the only solution to this problem.

Once one grasps these basic structural facts about modern societies, all talk of a "third way" between capitalism and socialism stands revealed as nonsensical. There is no "third way." There are, to be sure, modifications of the first and second "ways"—there are variants of capitalism, as there have been variants of socialism. And if one prefers to speak of a "mixed economy," every existing economy is "mixed" in the sense that it exhibits *some* combination of market forces and state interventions. In looking at these cases, as was noted above, it is useful to keep in mind the notion of the "commanding heights" of the economy. When one does that, it is rarely difficult to decide whether one is looking at a modification of the capitalist or the socialist "way." In current political parlance, though, "third way" rhetoric is not usually concerned with fine analytic distinctions. In Latin America, for example, it is typically the language of redistributionist populism, and it usually occurs in countries that can ill afford a lot of redistribution—*not* because the rich have so much that they will not give it up, but because the rich are few and do not have all that much to yield, so that redistribution means the destruction of the very middle class upon which economic growth depends. This "third way" is the Peronist model of development. Václav Klaus, the architect of the current capitalist experiment in the Czech and Slovak Federative Republic, put it very well when he observed that the third way is the fastest way to the Third World.

Thus the terms "capitalism" and "socialism" continue to be appropriate and useful. They refer to the two major alternative forms of economic organization in the contemporary world. As I have tried to indicate, though, these terms must not be taken as absolutes, but rather (to use Max Weber's phrase) as "ideal types" that approximate but do not fully represent empirical reality. It is also most useful to think here in terms of a continuum, the two extremes of which are empirically nonexistent. Somewhere in the middle of the continuum it may occasionally be difficult to decide which term to apply; most of the time, keeping in mind the concept of the "commanding heights," it is not difficult at all. (Hence, to repeat, social democracy, in the Scandinavian or any other form, is *not* a third model located somewhere outside the capitalist-socialist continuum.)

A Note of Caution

Considerations such as the ones I have been adducing have fueled the current mood of triumphalism among those who believe in democracy and capitalism. Since I share these beliefs, and since socialism has suffered an enormous defeat both intellectually and politically, I do not want to pour too much cold water on this happy mood. Nonetheless, a squirt or two of it might be in order.

⎮From an empirically and rationally rigorous point of view, the conclusion is indeed compelling that capitalism has shown an enduring capacity to produce historically unprecedented wealth and to allow huge masses of people to benefit from this. Socialism, on the contrary, wherever and whenever tried, has shown itself to be an unmitigated economic and political disaster. Moreover, the capitalist foundation that democracy requires seems to have been secured for the foreseeable future; democratic capitalism appears to be the only way to go.⎮

This line of thinking is well and good so far as it goes, but it all hinges on one highly questionable presupposition—namely, that the course of history is determined by the conclusions of rational minds. This presupposition, alas, is not one that experience recommends.

It is not hard to imagine scenarios that would make democratic capitalism very vulnerable indeed, especially in the societies that once comprised the Soviet Union and its satellites. These societies are now engaged in the gigantic and unprecedented experiment of trying to make the transition from a socialist to a capitalist economy. Not only is it amply clear that this transition will involve massive dislocations and suffering, at least in the short run, but we do not yet have either a full understanding of all its components or a set of sure policy prescriptions for managing it. For reasons already mentioned, it is not at all clear that democracy provides the optimal conditions for such a transition. Indeed, in a number of these countries "democracy" is at present little more than a thin veneer concealing older or newer versions of dictatorship. Where there is democracy in these societies, it would be foolhardy to bet that it will survive throughout the transition.

It is also far from certain that the transition will even occur in all these societies, under democratic or any other auspices. For many of those who are currently trying to dig themselves out from under the ruins of the "first socialist society in history," capitalism may quickly come to be associated with soaring inflation and unemployment, severe material hardships, the collapse of public order, and the advent of political chaos. Cool reasoning about the prospects of capitalism in the longer run will be of little comfort under such conditions. The entire shift to capitalism may then find itself stopped dead, while political rulers reimpose some variety of "emergency socialism" that might well become permanently institutionalized. In such a desperate scenario, even a return to the old Marxist-Leninist ideology cannot be totally ruled out, though no such explicit reversion would be required to reinstate the old socialist stagnation. A rhetoric of populist nationalism would be quite adequate for legitimating the reversal of what at present appears to some as an irreversible process.

Similarly bleak scenarios concerning the fate of democratic capitalism are possible in many of the less developed countries outside the postcommunist world that are now moving toward a market economy. Most of these countries probably have a little more time to show results than the ex-socialist societies. Their forms of statism or mercantilism have been less totally destructive than Soviet-style socialism; most of them have functioning capitalist institutions in at least some sectors of the economy; and their indigenous authoritarianisms have left some space for the dynamics of civil society. But even so, the costs of economic takeoff cannot be avoided; these costs will of necessity be unequally distributed; and the rhetoric of populism and nationalism is likely to fall on ready ears.

Again, in such situations of intense frustration rational arguments do not have much weight and few people are going to be interested in pondering the "lessons of history." There are no representatives of Sendero Luminoso participating in this symposium, and in the not unlikely event that Sendero Luminoso some day takes over in Peru, they certainly will not pay much heed to the kinds of arguments I have presented. It should also be borne in mind that, while socialism is highly irrational from the point of view of the well-being of a whole society, it can be very rational and lucrative for the socialist ruling elite. To use quasi-Marxist language, a command economy immiserates the masses, but it can very efficiently enrich the commanders. There are highly privileged ruling cliques, all more or less faithful replicas of the old Soviet *nomenklatura*, in charge of many Third World societies, and it is not easy to persuade *them* that socialism is economically irrational.

Last but not least, it is also premature to lay the ghost of Schumpeterian pessimism to rest in the advanced capitalist societies of Europe and North America. There continues to exist in these countries a Schumpeterian effect of bureaucracy seeking to stifle enterprise. There also remains a Schumpeterian "new class" (not his term, but he predicted the group to which it refers), and its basic instincts remain firmly anticapitalist. The womb that gave birth to Marxist utopianism is not yet barren. New utopian ideologies are springing up, kinder and gentler than Marxism perhaps, but capable of wreaking monumental economic havoc just the same. Thus there is a feminist path to socialism, and an environmentalist one. In both instances, the society proposed would feature dense thickets of entitlements and regulations that, in their aggregate, would add up to state control over the dynamics of the market and finally cause the latter's stagnation.

It is especially important to recall in this connection that no capitalist economy today exists in isolation from international competition. Economies that saddle themselves with a plethora of state interventions may lose decisive margins of comparative advantage vis-à-vis other economies less "sensitive" to the values legitimating such state interventions. To reiterate, we have no way of knowing at what precise point state intervention in a market economy will push the latter downward into a spiral of decline; we do know that there must be such a point, but by the time we discover it, it may well be too late.

I do not wish to conclude on a somber note, even though (like Schumpeter) I hail from the homeland of Central European pessimism. The last few years have indeed seen a series of triumphs for democratic capitalism, and its prospects today are much brighter than they have been for a very long time. Given my understanding of the economic features of modernity, I regard it as very unlikely that "new kinds of economic systems" will emerge in the foreseeable future (as the last question formulated for this symposium put it). Either capitalism will survive, or socialism will return in one form or another. If the latter eventuality occurs, the prospects for democracy are very gloomy indeed. On the other hand, if capitalism becomes the prevailing system in most if not all the world, then the prospects for democracy are quite bright. No sensible observer would want to say that the future of capitalism is assured. I do think, however, that one may be reasonably hopeful about this future, and therefore about the future of democracy, the less robust of these institutional twins.

2.
MARX, SCHUMPETER, AND THE EAST ASIAN EXPERIENCE

Kyung-won Kim

Kyung-won Kim *is president of the Institute of Social Sciences, a leading private research center in South Korea. He received his Ph.D. from Harvard University, and he has taught political science at Harvard, York University (Toronto), New York University, and Korea University. His publications include* Revolution and the International System *(1970). He has also held important government posts, including ambassador to the United Nations and ambassador to the United States.*

As the twentieth century approaches its end, we are witnessing two epoch-making historical developments. Contrary to the expectations of both socialists and their opponents, the socialist regimes in Eastern Europe and the former Soviet Union have collapsed swiftly and thoroughly, and without any external cause such as war.[1] Perhaps less surprisingly, but also against the predictions of most experts, modernizing authoritarian regimes with successful market economies, particularly in East Asia, have begun to evolve into democracies.

Both developments have profound implications for the relations among capitalism, socialism, and democracy. They also suggest the possibility that we may be entering the age of democracy. In order to comprehend fully the meaning of these recent historical developments, however, we must pause to consider the theories that predicted the opposite of what actually happened.

Communism at its philosophical core amounted to a belief that man could not fulfill his humanity unless society was transformed so as to liberate him from all individual acquisitiveness. In a sense, communism was as much an ideology of freedom as liberalism. Where it differed from liberalism was in its belief that man could obtain true freedom only through the absolute destruction of all structures of inequality.[2]

The failure of communism, therefore, calls into question the notion that the utter denial of man's acquisitive urge is a necessary condition for the actualization of man's freedom. Indeed, this failure suggests that the exact opposite—namely, the acknowledgment of man's acquisitive drive as an inherent part of human nature—may be among the conditions necessary for a free society.

The collapse of communism across the former Soviet bloc can be attributed to two seemingly separate but actually interrelated causes: the failure of centrally planned command economies, and rising citizen demands for greater freedom. A condition of equality did not "liberate" man from the acquisitive urge any more than the abolition of private property led to genuine equality. Nor did outlawing private ownership of the means of production solve the problem of scarcity, as communists believed it would. The abolition of private property led to enormous inefficiencies, making the frustration of the acquisitive instinct much sharper and more urgently felt.

Communism's fall compels us to ask anew about the relationship between democracy and socialism. We can no longer feel confident that, as Joseph Schumpeter suggested 50 years ago, there is no relationship, either positive or negative, between socialism and democracy. The rejection of the former in the name of the latter may not by itself demonstrate a necessarily hostile relationship between the two, but it does raise the fundamental question of the relations between a political system and an economic system.

Marx's Mistake

It was Karl Marx who first raised the question of political democracy's compatibility with a particular economic system. Like most socialists, Marx believed that democracy was not only compatible with socialism but necessarily linked to it. For him, both democracy and socialism stood for freedom. Since socialism meant an economic system in which structural inequalities have been permanently "overcome," it was the only basis on which the political superstructure of true democracy could stand.

The assumptions on which Marx based his thesis about the necessary relationship between democracy and socialism led logically to his rejection of capitalism as an economic system incompatible with democracy. The state under capitalism, Marx said, is nothing more than "the executive committee of the exploiting class," and hence cannot possibly be democratic. The "exploiting class" in a capitalist society holds the power to exploit by virtue of its ownership of the means of production. Those who are excluded from control over these means can never hope to compete with the capitalist class on an equal footing. From the Marxian perspective, "bourgeois" democracy is a sham.

Yet Marx's assertion that communism would automatically usher in democracy raises questions even within the context of his own theory. By abolishing private property, communism would by definition eliminate the capitalist instrument of exploitation. There would no longer be a permanent ruling class for whom bourgeois democracy provided the state apparatus as an exploitive instrument. But Marx never claimed that the communist transformation would occur in an instant. Capitalism's inner contradictions would take time to manifest themselves and become unbearable. The bourgeois class would have to shrink and finally crumble. Only at the end of a considerable period of transition would a postcapitalist society reach the stage of communism.

The transitional postcapitalist society, Marx recognized, could not be a democracy, as remaining contradictions would still need to be eliminated. In fact, to ensure the transition's continuance, Marx was prepared to entrust the task of midwifing democracy to what he called "the revolutionary dictatorship of the proletariat."[3] In effect this meant (as Lenin saw) that the party "representing" the proletariat would hold unrivaled sway over the state.

But what guarantee could there be that this proletarian party, once in total control of the state, would cede power? By democracy, Marx surely did not mean a political system of checks and balances. On the contrary, by assuming that a communist society would be free from all social contradictions, Marx "solved" the problem of restraining political power by theoretically eliminating the need for any such restraint. At the same time, however, he could not evade the problem of democratic transition, because even he did not equate "the dictatorship of the proletariat" with democracy.

Marx may have thought that once the inequalities inherent in the capitalist system had been eliminated, the rulers during the ensuing transitional stage would act without the selfishness characteristic of acquisitive "bourgeois" man. Such an argument would be in the tradition of Rousseauan romanticism: strip away social conventions, and man will reveal himself as an unselfish, compassionate being. Yet Marx's dilemma is that the transitional stage is still a transitional stage. Enough old social conventions will linger to require absolute party control over the state. Eventually, the state as an instrument of the bourgeoisie will "wither away." In the meantime, Marx is prepared to recognize the need for the state to become an instrument serving the party of the proletariat.

Ultimately, Marx had no answer to the problem of how the dictatorship of the proletariat would transform itself into a democracy. That is why those who claimed to have been inspired by him decided to rechristen the dictatorship of the proletariat "people's democracy." They must have sensed that if they had to wait until the end of party control before they could claim democracy, they would have to wait indefinitely. Proclaiming that the democratic transition had already been completed must have seemed a better strategy.

Marx himself would never have mistaken one of these bogus "people's democracies" for the ideal democracy that he originally envisioned. The tragedy of Marx's democratic vision is that his lofty aspirations wound up legitimating stubborn dictatorships rather than sweeping socialist transformations.

The current debacle of communism is a necessary result of the logic of Marxian social-transformation theory. The dictatorship of the proletariat possesses no inherent tendency to evolve into democracy. Introducing freedom thus meant breaking the dictatorship of the communist party. Socialism in the form of the dictatorship of the proletariat (institutionally incarnated as one-party rule) was plainly incompatible with democracy.

Schumpeter's Simplification

Joseph Schumpeter, of course, did not have "people's democracy" or the dictatorship of the proletariat in mind when he declared that socialism was compatible with democracy. When he wrote that "there is no necessary relation" between socialism and democracy, he was careful to specify that he meant "socialism as we defined it and democracy as we defined it."[4]

Schumpeter defined "socialist society" as "an institutional pattern in which the control over means of production and over production itself is vested with a central authority" (p. 167). Compared to what Marx understood by socialism, this is a rather spare definition, stripped of what Schumpeter must have regarded as unnecessary philosophical baggage. In fact, Schumpeter speaks of the "cultural indeterminateness of socialism," by which he means that if one does not accept Marx's economic determinism, one cannot posit any necessary relationship between socialism, which is an economic concept, and any noneconomic phenomena—democracy or dictatorship, asceticism or hedonism, nationalism or internationalism (p. 170). Ever a model of fairness, Schumpeter admitted that "cultural indeterminateness" applies to capitalism as well. In other words, he saw his thesis that socialism and capitalism are both compatible with democracy as following logically from his rejection of the Marxist view that economics determines everything else, including politics.

Schumpeter's definition of democracy was as lean as his definition of socialism. Rejecting the "classical" conception of democracy on the grounds that the "common good," which the classical theory takes as its focus, actually does not exist (at least not in any generally discernable form), Schumpeter reduced democracy to "that institutional arrangement for arriving at political decisions in which individuals acquire the power to decide by means of a comprehensive struggle for the people's vote" (p. 269). His intention here is the same as in his definition of socialism—namely, to strip away all needless substantive content in order to arrive at a "value-free" functional specification without any philosophical or teleological trappings. Democracy is no longer understood in terms of some political good such as freedom, equality, or "the greatest happiness of the greatest number." For a society to be called democratic, it is enough that those in power be elected to their positions "by means of a comprehensive struggle for the people's vote."

As long as the definitions of socialism and democracy that Schumpeter proposes are not logically related to each other, he is right to aver that there is no "necessary" relation between the two. At the same time, if we are willing to grant Schumpeter the right to deduce his proposition of "no necessary relation" from the definitions he has posited, we are also entitled to conclude that this proposition is not a statement about the empirical world, which exists independently of his definitions.

In the empirical world, "democracy" is generally taken to mean a good deal more than just a system of competitive electoral politics. The institution of free elections must be situated within a political system that guarantees the freedoms of individuals against arbitrary uses of state power. The precise list of freedoms to be guaranteed and their exact scope are not subjects of universal agreement, of course. Indeed, debate about just these questions is the very stuff of democratic theory.

Schumpeter's own fundamental definition was meant to preclude any such debate by omitting all references to individual freedom or any other "good" that democracy is commonly supposed to maximize. By reducing the meaning of democracy to competitive electoral politics, Schumpeter believed that he had eliminated all the ambiguities inherent in the classical theory of democracy.

The urge to eliminate ambiguity is understandable. But if a political concept is artificially rendered unambiguous by emptying it of analytically "unnecessary" normative content, the resulting definition may wind up being devoid of what all ordinary usage takes to be the concept's very essence. The commonsense understanding of democracy regards competitive elections as a means of achieving the end of democratic politics, which is the protection of individual freedom. By disconnecting the means from all consideration of the end that the means were originally and generally thought to serve, Schumpeter turned democracy into an institutional form bereft of any substance. More seriously still, his attempt to eliminate all ambiguity from the definition of democracy led to new and even less tractable difficulties.

If electoral competition is the sole requirement for democracy, all those who gain power as a result of electoral victory must be considered democrats. But such is not the case in real life. Zviad Gamsakhurdia is hardly a democrat, although he was elected president of Georgia. The Islamic Salvation Front (FIS) won the recent elections in Algeria before the country's military suspended the electoral process in order to prevent the rise of an FIS government. One need not approve of this coup d'état in order to suspect that had the FIS come to power, it would hardly have behaved in accord with democratic norms. To accept Schumpeter's definition would lead one into the absurd position of insisting that all manner of dictators were indeed democrats merely by virtue of having been somehow "elected."

Another problem with Schumpeter's definition arises when a political system holds elections that always leave the same political party in power. In the absence of power transfer between contending parties, particularly when the ruling party looks permanently entrenched in power, how meaningful is the formal process of electoral competition?

Japan exemplifies the dominant-party system. The country is governed by a permanent alliance between the Liberal Democratic Party and the state bureaucracy that effectively blocks any meaningful voter influence on public policy. Marx would probably join the many current observers, including Japanese commentators, who have asked whether it makes sense to call this arrangement democracy. Yet Japanese citizens do enjoy a wide range of freedoms, certainly more than are enjoyed by people in most other dominant-party systems.[5] Singapore has a more pronounced dominant-party system. Yet it cannot be denied that, at least in institutional form, politicians in Singapore "acquire the power to decide by means of a comprehensive struggle for the people's vote." If Japan (as most observers would agree) is closer to being a full-fledged democracy than Singapore, it cannot be because one has the "institutional arrangement" for elections while the other does not. It must rather be because Japan's political system allows more freedom than does Singapore's.

Severing the concept of democracy from democracy's traditional concern for the protection of individual freedom only creates new ambiguities. These ambiguities are such that defining democracy purely in terms of electoral competition does not help us make distinctions between the more and less democratic systems which common sense tells us do exist in the real world.

Limiting the Sphere of Public Authority

When we turn to Schumpeter's discussion of the conditions that make possible "the success of the democratic method," we discover that his full understanding of democracy was far richer and closer to the commonsense view than one might suppose, given his earlier and rather aridly formal definition of democratic government. Among the conditions that Schumpeter cited, the importance of what he called "a large measure of tolerance for difference of opinion" figures prominently. When Schumpeter wrote that "the human material of [democratic] politics . . . should be of sufficiently high quality"; that "the effective range of political decision should not be extended too far"; that there must be "a well-trained bureaucracy of good standing and tradition"; and that "democratic self-control" is imperative, he was not thinking of these as conditions necessary for the formal existence of competitive elections (pp. 289-96). He knew that democracy meant protecting the sphere of individual freedom, which in turn meant limiting the sphere of politics while maintaining a climate of tolerance and self-restraint. This understanding enabled him to realize that, despite his assertion of the logical equality of capitalism and socialism as far as democracy was concerned, capitalism actually had a unique and positive relationship with democracy that socialism did not. He wrote:

> The bourgeoisie has a solution that is peculiar to it for the problem of how the sphere of political decision can be reduced to those proportions which are manageable by means of the method of competitive leadership. The bourgeois scheme of things limits the sphere of politics by limiting the sphere of public authority: its solution is in the ideal of the parsimonious state that exists primarily in order to guarantee bourgeois legality and to provide a firm frame for autonomous individual endeavor in all fields (p. 297).

Fully aware of "the consequences of extending the democratic method, that is to say the sphere of 'politics,' to all economic affairs," Schumpeter nonetheless held that a socialist state could preserve democracy by refusing to extend the sphere of public authority beyond a certain limit. As he gamely put it:

> Extension of the range of public management does not imply corresponding extension of the range of political management. Conceivably, the former may be extended so as to absorb a nation's economic affairs while the latter still remains within the boundaries set by the limitations of the democratic method (p. 299).

Schumpeter's liberal temperament led him to see clearly that democracy means limiting government in order to allow sufficient room for "autonomous individual endeavor." Although he thought that the decline of capitalism and the eventual rise of socialism were inevitable, he was unhappy about the prospect.[6] His attempt to show that the triumph of socialism need not spell the death of democracy reads less like the prophecy of a true believer than the prayer of a man who knows how what he fears most can come to pass.

If democracy is possible only when political power is limited to make way for autonomous individual endeavor, what can provide such room for initiative when private persons have no control over the means of production? Socialists are the first to argue that control over the means of production is the key to political power. In a socialist system, these means are firmly in the hands of the central authority; it is idle to hope, as Schumpeter does, that "the range of political management" will remain "within the boundaries set by the limitations of the democratic method." One could say that Schumpeter's vision of democratic socialism is, in an ironic sense, no less "utopian" than Marx's.

All things considered, then, Schumpeter's views point to the conclusion that socialism (defined as state control of the means of production) is most unlikely to be a fertile ground for democracy. In this most crucial respect, Schumpeter's dilemma is no different from Marx's. Once each of them defined socialism as a system of public monopoly over the most important power resources, the only way he could claim that this monopoly would not lead to dictatorship was to suggest that somehow the powerholders would exercise tremendous self-restraint even in the absence of any serious opposition.

History shows, however, that democracy emerged out of a dialectic of opposition between competing forces, not thanks to the good will of potentates. It was the rise of the bourgeoisie that led to the placement of limits on the traditional power structures of feudalism or royal absolutism. Like the communist bosses centuries after them, the rulers of the precapitalist *ancien régime* did not freely yield power; they had to be forced into giving it up. The process was more gradual and less violent in some nations than in others, but the pattern has been the same in every successful democracy. All of them have seen the rise of a social class deriving its living from commercial, industrial, or professional pursuits rather than traditionally agrarian sources. Since the state was tied to privileges based on birth and the landed economy, it was only natural that the new bourgeois groups should seek to limit state power. The democratic polity, in other words, sprang from the womb of the capitalist economy.

Authoritarian Modernization

We should not, however, posit the complete identity of democracy and capitalism. As Ralf Dahrendorf has shown, capitalist development did not invariably lead to democracy.[7] Particularly in the case of Germany under the Second Reich (1870-1918), industrialization did not give rise to a politically cohesive and assertive middle class, but instead allowed the existing ruling structure to absorb into its own ranks the most talented and ambitious members of the bourgeoisie.

Because Germany's industrialization came rather late and was carried out as a matter of deliberate state policy, it was extraordinarily thorough. From the beginning, German industry was dominated by large-scale enterprises, some of them (such as railroads, mines, and port facilities) state-owned. There was little room left over for medium-sized and small businesses. Consequently, the sort of ambitious mercantile class that had appeared in most other West European states by the second half of the nineteenth century failed to emerge in Germany on any significant scale. Moreover, whatever Germany did have in the way of a bourgeoisie owed its success to the protection and guidance of the state. To expect such a state-dependent class to make bold political claims would have been fanciful. Bismarck further strengthened the state by giving it social welfare functions. Yet as Dahrendorf reminds us, what the Germans had was not a liberal democracy, but an authoritarian welfare state.

What is troubling about Germany's experience is that despite the state's crucial role, the German economy under the Second Reich could only be described as capitalist. Clearly, we cannot argue that a capitalist economy always leads to a democratic polity. The German case shows that when capitalist industrialization is initiated and guided by the state instead of by a politically autonomous bourgeoisie, an authoritarian regime can preempt the rise of liberal democracy by coopting or diverting those groups that would otherwise press for democracy.

This insight, derived from a European case, caused some observers to suggest that since today's modernizing societies are led by technical-cum-bureaucratic elites rather than by independent elements in civil society, modernization brings with it not liberal democracy but "bureaucratic authoritarianism."[8] This theory has found its most receptive audience among students of South America and East Asia.

To most scholars of development, the failure of economic modernization to produce political modernization—implicitly or explicitly understood as democratization in some broad sense—was a puzzle demanding explanation. Even those who rejected the Marxist paradigm still expected economic change to be accompanied by related political change; how then could modernizing nations continue to be ruled by authoritarian regimes?

As Dahrendorf discovered in the case of Bismarckian and Wilhelmine Germany, students of bureaucratic authoritarianism in the post-1945 world report that authoritarian elites in modernizing societies can succeed by embracing modernization as their own program. The pursuit of modernization through industrialization need no longer be a hit-or-miss affair with no guiding hand save perhaps an invisible one, but may become the very *raison d'être* of the ruling elite. Authoritarianism in modernizing societies thus generally eschews appeals to "irrational"—charismatic or traditional—types of authority, and aspires instead to bureaucratic or technocratic "rationality."

The implications are evident. Since modernization in the developing countries of noncommunist Asia is the project of a bureaucratic-authoritarian elite rather than an independent middle class, it is futile to expect such nations to evolve into pluralistic democracies on their own. Barring the intervention of exogenous traumas like defeat in war and foreign occupation (the "Japanese solution"), there seems to be little prospect of the bureaucratic-authoritarian regime transforming itself into a democratic one.

Some theorists have gone further and tried to prove that today's non-

European industrializing nations cannot help but remain authoritarian.[9] Industrialization requires a concentrated process of capital accumulation through increased saving. In Western Europe, these theorists maintain, favorable circumstances made it possible to achieve capital accumulation without violently suppressing labor. No such good fortune, however, smiles on today's developing nations. The only way for them to accumulate capital rapidly enough to pursue industrialization is by ruthlessly holding down the wages paid to labor. In such a situation, labor can never hope to acquire enough independence to become an autonomous political force. The idea of a free labor movement remains only a dream, and civil society in general remains too stunted to challenge the overweening state.

A theory purporting to explain why today's developing nations cannot help but have authoritarian governments appeals to both defenders and critics of such regimes. To the former, it provides a rationale showing that authoritarian rule is "necessary." For critics, it explains why it is futile to expect democracy to arise gradually from an authoritarian regime. Rapid, deliberate, and concentrated industrialization is inimical to democracy. Somewhat improbably, many such critics seem to suggest that only by eschewing economic development can today's Third World nations expect to become democracies.

The Case of East Asia

The recent historical record, it is heartening to note, does not support such pessimism. In East Asia, for instance, nations that have pursued industrialization under authoritarian regimes have undergone democratic evolution without exogenous traumas. Notable examples are South Korea and, to a more limited extent, Taiwan, both of which display features of what Robert Scalapino calls the authoritarian-pluralist system.[10]

Surveying all of East and South Asia since the end of the Second World War, Scalapino discerns three types of regimes. The first type, found in China, North Korea, and Vietnam, features a Leninist one-party system in which not only politics but economic affairs and society as a whole are tightly regulated from the top. The second type, Scalapino's "authoritarian-pluralist" regime, "accepts or even encourages economic and social pluralism" but relies on authoritarian control to maintain political unity. It is bureaucratic authoritarianism under another name, combining undemocratic politics with a market-oriented economy. The third type is liberal democracy, found in Japan and former British colonies such as Malaysia, Singapore, and India.

An important question here is whether there is any significant difference between Leninism and the authoritarian-pluralist system when it comes to prospects for democratization. Recent history indicates that there is, and that authoritarian pluralism is superior.

Apart from ideology, rapid mass communications have probably had the most profound impact on the history of our time. The technology of information—fax machines, copiers, radio and television, and personal computers—is making nation-states increasingly porous. Territorial impermeability, long considered an essential condition of state sovereignty, is no longer an operative reality. The collapse of communism in Eastern Europe and the former Soviet Union had many causes, but growing access to information about the world beyond their borders certainly played a key role in persuading the people of those lands to throw off the Leninist yoke.

When it comes to blocking information from the "capitalist" world, the Leninist regimes of Asia have shown themselves much readier to resort to harsh measures than their erstwhile counterparts in the former USSR and Eastern Europe. Asia's Leninists face a dilemma, for the only real way to keep the curtains drawn is to forgo all economic links to the outside world. But the price of political unity achieved through information denial—as the case of North Korea testifies—is economic stagnation, technological backwardness, and permanent underdevelopment.

China under Deng Xiaoping, however, has been experimenting with what Beijing may well regard as its own "third way." Fully aware of the disastrous consequences of economic isolation, especially when combined with rigid, doctrinaire state management, China's reformers decided to open the country's economy to the outside world and also to introduce certain features of the market economy.

Economic success, however, has come at a political cost to the regime. Beijing hoped to limit interactions with the outside world to the strictly economic sphere, but as China's communist rulers might have recalled from their youthful reading of Marx, the economy and society are inseparably intertwined, and together help shape politics. The tragedy of Tiananmen was, in a way, a foregone conclusion.

What is remarkable about the Chinese situation is that, once Chinese leaders committed themselves to a program of economic modernization, they had no real alternative but to transform their system into a version of authoritarian pluralism. To be sure, the transformation still has a long way to go. Yet as long as China continues introducing market processes, decontrolling prices, and privatizing production, it is bound to become more pluralist in its economic and social aspects. Ideology will probably keep receiving lip service, as Chinese leaders, in their quintessentially Chinese way, deal with contradictions between rhetoric and practice by repeating the official catechism about "socialism with Chinese characteristics" as if they really believed that a problem could be chased away by "rectification of names." North Korea now seems to be moving toward adopting the Chinese solution. If Pyongyang continues down this road, North Korea too will become an authoritarian-pluralist state. Eventually, after many tactical retreats and detours, North Korea will probably go through the same kind of process that occurred in South Korea.

Whereas in Eastern Europe and the former Soviet Union communism simply collapsed and in doing so opened up possibilities for democratization, the communist regime in China is transforming itself into a de facto authoritarian-pluralist system in order to meet the demands of modernization. In both cases, however, communism in the sense of tight central control over the entire ensemble of productive means and economic processes had to be ended before democratic possibilities could appear on the horizon. In other words, the recent crisis of communism shows that it is incompatible with democracy. The problem inherent in Marx's theory—namely, the improbability of the dictatorship of the proletarian party voluntarily dissolving itself in order to give rise to democracy—has now been amply demonstrated by the most costly political experiment of this or perhaps any century.

China's future depends on the relationship between authoritarian pluralism and democracy. Earlier, we suggested that the concept of authoritarian pluralism traces back to the concept of bureaucratic authoritarianism, which in turn traces back to the notion of state-directed capitalism as described by scholars like Ralf Dahrendorf and Barrington Moore. Behind this line of analysis lies the view that capitalist industrialization, when primed and orchestrated "from above" by the state rather than initiated and led "from below" by the autonomous bourgeoisie, leads to nondemocratic outcomes.

Recent developments in Asia suggest something else as well. Certainly, the authoritarian-pluralist regime is not democratic in either its character or its aims. On the contrary, to the extent that such a regime has at its disposal all the coercive and persuasive capabilities of a modern bureaucratic state, its authoritarianism is not likely to be distinguished by exceptional mildness. As the records show in South Korea and Taiwan, a bureaucratic-authoritarian regime can be as politically harsh as any other dictatorial regime while allowing or even encouraging social and economic pluralism. Yet by encouraging such pluralism—by fostering capitalism, in other words—the authoritarian-pluralist regime is either wittingly or unwittingly making possible the emergence of a middle class. To the extent that the state's modernization policies succeed, this class, born in the womb of capitalism, will grow in size and weight. Eventually, it will begin making political claims against the authoritarian regime. All studies on the subject in Korea show that the number of those who identified themselves as members of the middle class grew dramatically during the 1970s and 1980s, years of intense industrialization overseen by a bureaucratic-authoritarian regime headed by former generals. By mid-1987, the regime could no longer contain the demands of this new group within the confines of the old authoritarian structure. The mass uprising that broke out in June of that year, and the regime's subsequent decision to yield power and accept a more democratic constitution, were inevitable consequences of a process that the government itself had set in train. In encouraging economic pluralism, the regime had been digging its own grave.

The gain for South Korea was enormous. For the first time, democracy became a real (indeed, perhaps the only) possibility rather than just a fleeting mirage brought to sight by the heat of dramatic events, as was certainly the case in the spring of 1960. The country still has a long and arduous road to travel before it can be called a mature democracy, but the journey has begun. The authoritarian-pluralist regime, knowingly or not, set the wheels in motion, chiefly by fostering the "capitalist" character of Korea's economy and society.

It is in the nature of capitalism that it secretly nurtures and eventually unleashes democratic forces. When capitalism itself is a product of historical conditions in which the industrial bourgeoisie makes its appearance as the foe of the feudal-aristocratic state, democracy is the immediate outcome of the capitalist revolution. In a late-industrializing society, however, the state tends to adopt industrialization as its own program. In the absence of an autonomous bourgeoisie, the immediate consequence of state-directed industrialization is usually authoritarianism. But even an authoritarian industrializing state—unless it opts for an absolute command economy, as Leninist regimes did—will eventually find itself contending with democratic forces unleashed by an assertive middle class that the state itself has indirectly fostered.

Socialism, on the other hand, is clearly incompatible with democracy. The state's monopoly of the economic sphere leaves little or no room for an autonomous oppositional force within the institutional structure of the regime. Claims against the central authority can be made only in a revolutionary mode, since there is no space within official public life for criticism or opposition. It is not by accident that decisive political change in Eastern Europe and the former USSR could occur only as a revolutionary negation of the socialist system itself, and not as its evolutionary modification.

Postideological Democracy

Socialism that falls short of complete domination of the economy by the central government is a different matter. As Schumpeter said of those European socialists, particularly in Britain and Germany, who decided after World War I to take part in bourgeois parliamentary politics, sharing or sometimes even holding power, they were not exactly behaving in the manner that Marx had in mind when he called on the workers of the world to unite. They were in fact operating in "a social and economic system that would not function except on capitalist lines" (p. 364). They might do many things within such a system in order to control and regulate it in the interests of labor. What they could not and did not even try to do was turn it into socialism. Instead, they settled for being able to "administer capitalism." That is why socialists in power, as long as they do not try to convert the system into a socialist one in the strict sense, pose no threat to democracy. Even nationalization of major industries, progressive taxation, and active welfare programs need not destroy capitalism. Indeed, they may under certain circumstances even help to save democracy by saving capitalism from the destructive consequences of pursuing its own logic too relentlessly.

A capitalism that can be administered by socialists is, of course, a different kind of capitalism from what many of its strongest proponents believe it should be. Yet capitalism's roots do not lie in doctrinal pronouncements. On the contrary, in the history of capitalism, practice has always preceded theory. Capitalism as an ideology is a response to the appearance of socialism. Considered in itself, capitalism is a nonideological phenomenon; that is why socialists can administer it, regulate it, and modify it without capitalism ceasing to be capitalism.

When socialist politicians first took on the job of managing a capitalist economy, observers should have realized that the age of ideology was at an end. In the event, however, almost a half century would pass before any declarations to that effect were heard. Socialism as a Romantic revolutionary doctrine, trumpeting man's deliverance from the dehumanizing compulsions of an acquisitive industrial society, died before it could be born. From the beginning, the ideological competition between capitalism and socialism was really no contest, both because capitalism has never really been about ideology and because socialism in the strict sense has always been a chimera, an all-too-ideological creature that can never take on flesh.

All this has become especially evident today. The collapse of communism leaves no room for socialism in its doctrinally pure form, while the cumulative experience of procapitalist governments that have inherited and managed programs inaugurated by "socialist" predecessors makes doctrinaire antisocialist capitalism seem less and less relevant. This is not to say that there will not continue to be plenty for the left and right to argue about. In some cases the degree of state control over the economy may come perilously close to the limit beyond which the vitality of democracy can be seriously impaired. By the same token, the market may be left so unattended as to create social and economic dislocations that seriously threaten the stability of democracy. These two extremes aside, however, striking the right equilibrium has become an essentially technical exercise.

We are entering an age of postideological democracy. Socialism is no longer a threat to democracy, for socialism cannot survive the inevitable collapse of socialist economic systems. Authoritarian-pluralist regimes, meanwhile, should continue to be undone by their own successes.

The age of democracy does not necessarily represent the ultimate fulfillment of humanity's highest aspirations. Yet to judge the age of democracy from the standpoint of the presumed virtues of predemocratic society is to miss the point completely. History has progressed to the democratic epoch not because men longed only for wealth and consumer comfort, but because they cared passionately about freedom from the oppression inflicted on them by despotic rulers, be they feudal, authoritarian, or Leninist. True enough, the disappearance of oppressive authorities takes away the reason for passion and commitment. But it would be naive to think that democracy by itself can guarantee the permanent absence of all actual and potential sources of oppression. There will continue to be plenty to guard against. Democracy, instead of being the ultimate fulfillment of all that is best in man, is now making it possible—for the first time in history—for every person to struggle toward that fulfillment. The age of democracy does not mark the close of that struggle. In many ways, it is only the beginning of that existential drama for every individual.

NOTES

1. In this essay the term "socialism," unless qualified, is used in the same sense as "communism." Both are understood to mean the ideology which advocates a system of complete "collective" ownership of the productive means and processes. Socialists who do not aim at complete collectivization are referred to as socialists in the qualified sense.

2. For an exploration of the ramifications, many of them profoundly disturbing, of the kind of freedom that Marx meant, one could do no better than to read Sir Isaiah Berlin's Oxford Inaugural Lecture on "Two Concepts of Liberty," in his, *Four Essays on Liberty* (London: Oxford University Press, 1969), 118-72.

3. Karl Marx, "Critique of the Gotha Programme," in Robert C. Tucker, ed., *The Marx-Engels Reader*, 2nd ed. (New York: W.W. Norton, 1978), 538.

4. Joseph A. Schumpeter, *Capitalism, Socialism and Democracy*, 3rd ed. (New York: Harper and Row, 1950), 284. For all subsequent citations of this work, page numbers will appear in the text.

5. Robert A. Scalapino, *The Politics of Development: Perspectives on Twentieth-Century Asia* (Cambridge: Harvard University Press, 1989), 62.

6. For a superb introduction to Schumpeter and his world, see Thomas K. McGraw, "Schumpeter Ascending," *The American Scholar* 60 (Summer 1991): 371-92.

7. Ralf Dahrendorf, *Society and Democracy in Germany* (New York: Doubleday, 1969). Cf. Barrington Moore, *Social Origins of Dictatorship and Democracy* (Boston: Beacon Press, 1966).

8. For a representative statement of this view, see Guillermo O'Donnell, *Modernization and Bureaucratic Authoritarianism* (Berkeley, Calif.: Institute of International Studies, 1972).

9. Karl de Schweinitz, *Industrialization and Democracy* (New York: Free Press of Glencoe, 1964).

10. Scalapino, op. cit., 71-131.

3.
DEVALUING DEMOCRACY

Claude Ake

Claude Ake *is director of the Center for Advanced Social Science and a member and the former dean of the faculty of social sciences of the University of Port Harcourt, Nigeria. He is a former president of the Council for the Development of Economic and Social Research, the umbrella social science organization in Africa. He has recently been a fellow at both the Brookings Institution and the Woodrow Wilson International Center for Scholars. His books include* A Theory of Political Integration *(1967),* The Theory of Political Development *(1982), and* A Political Economy of Africa *(1982).*

For the sake of clarity and convenience, our subject may be divided into two basic questions, the first of which is relatively simple, while the second is markedly difficult, though perhaps unnecessarily so.

First, the easier question: Is socialism or capitalism the more productive *economic* system? The answer would appear to be capitalism, judging from the phenomenal prosperity of the West and the recent demise of the Soviet empire, which collapsed less because of pressures for democratization (though they surely played a role) than because of economic crisis. Yet we should also take into account the extraordinary rise of the Soviet Union from a backward feudal country to superpower status, as well as the "capitalist encirclement" in the face of which the Soviet Union, standing alone against the alliance of all the advanced Western countries, was forced to dissipate its energies in wasteful competition. Would the Soviet Union have suffered economic collapse in a less hostile international environment and with better economic management? We will never know.

In any case, the present reality is that the West continues to prosper; it is the Soviet Union and its allies that have collapsed economically. More significantly, they have not seen their collapse as a temporary setback that is still reversible under socialism. Rather, they appear to be convinced that they cannot repair their economic decline without embracing the market. So, for this historical juncture, and on this subjective level, we can say that the evidence is in—capitalism has emerged as the more successful economic system.

Since it is now the fashion to conclude that socialist theory was wrong about everything, it is well to note that this theory never had any doubts about the vitality and productivity of capitalism. Over and over again, Marx underlined its dynamism, its inevitable march to globalization, and its prodigious productivity; indeed, he was so impressed by capitalism's achievements that he represented it as the guarantor of the material base of modern civilization. That is why capitalism was necessary even in Europe's colonies, where its savagery was given free rein. What socialist theory questioned was not the productivity of capitalism but its sustainability in the face of the contradictions that it engendered. The theory predicted that in the long run, these contradictions would overwhelm it. But if the present health of capitalism is any guide, the "long run" will be very long indeed.

Popular Power versus Liberal Democracy

Now for the difficult question: Is capitalism or socialism the better system *politically*, in the sense of being more conducive to democracy? The answer to this question, so often asked, continues to elude us. More often than not, attempts to answer it only compound our confusion. This is not unconnected to tendencies, regrettably discernible in the essays of Peter Berger and Kyung-won Kim, to appropriate democratic legitimacy to historical "democratic" practice, and to conflate democracy as such with liberal democracy. Once this conflation is made, the correlation between capitalism and democracy is easily established, but only on the basis of an assumption that devalues democracy to the point of jeopardizing its status as an emancipatory project.

The issue here is not simply one of differing definitions of democracy. For in this case, the definitions are stakes in a bitter political contest. Actually, the meaning of democracy is perfectly clear. For a political concept, it is uncharacteristically precise. Democracy means popular power, rule by the *demos*. That is how the Greeks, who invented both the word and the practice, understood it. Popular power also lay at the heart of the democratic theory of the French Revolution, which launched the modern polity. It remains the classic definition of democracy, restated with poignant simplicity by a famous American as "government of the people, by the people, for the people."

Popular power was threatening to some interests, and it was these interests who started redefining democracy in order to deradicalize it. It was they who complexified its meaning. Opposition to democracy was taken up by the rising European bourgeoisie, horrified by the radical democratic egalitarianism that the French Revolution had so vividly displayed. In the end, the bourgeoisie succeeded in replacing democracy with "liberal" democracy, which was not so much a political morality as an economic convenience—the political correlate of the market, necessary for optimizing its sustainability and efficiency.

The relationship of liberal democracy to capitalism has been demonstrated by social contract theorists like Hobbes and Locke. They have shown that the type of political association that would be voluntarily instituted by people who are attentive to their interests as property owners is liberal democracy—a regime that essentially bans the state from acting as an entrepreneur, makes the state financially dependent on its subjects, holds the right to property inviolable, places emphasis on the individual rather than the collectivity, and values the rule of law. It is markedly democratic, but it is not democracy.

It is easier now to see the problems that lurk in the analyses offered by Berger and Kim. They both come down on the side of conventional wisdom, arguing that capitalism is necessary for democracy, and that only capitalist systems can be democratic; at the same time, they acknowledge that capitalist systems are not necessarily democratic, especially in the earlier stages of their development, when authoritarian rule appears to be an asset.

The first point they make—that only capitalist systems can be democratic—does not tell us very much; it is only formally true, in as much as they reduce democracy to liberal democracy. By the same token, their second point, which stresses that capitalist systems need not be democratic, is rooted in confusion. It leads them to embrace a false, albeit popular, conception regarding capitalist development and democracy in South Korea, Taiwan, and Japan. There is no problem, goes this line of argument, in explaining how these countries failed at first to be democratic, or how, once having achieved capitalist development, they had to become democratic: At the beginning of their industrialization, they were not capitalist systems (or better yet "market societies"), except in a rudimentary sense. As they evolved into capitalist systems proper, they became *ipso facto* liberal democracies, for what is liberal democracy if not the political correlate of capitalist production?

It is misleading to imply, as these essays do, that democracy is a simple good which is either present or absent. Democracy is better conceived of as a complex range of possibilities of form and content. If we avoid the mistake of conflating democracy with liberal democracy, it is easier to see democratic possibilities in a broader range of productive systems than is dreamt of in Berger's or Kim's philosophies. Capitalism is admittedly one type of democratic possibility because it bases government on the consent of the governed and insists on freedom, the guarantee of rights, the rule of law, and the taming of the state. It has a down side too, though, for under capitalism rights tend to be abstract rather than concrete, the consent of the governed is usually taken rather than given, and an unduly high tolerance of inequality compromises the liberties of some or even most citizens. It is often said that for all its problems, liberal democracy may well be the best political system that we can have. But we cannot possibly know with certainty that it is the best we can have. Therefore, we must resist the urge to idealize it, and must instead strive to improve it.

The Democratic Possibilities of Socialism

Professor Kim denies socialism any democratic potential, pronouncing it "clearly incompatible with political democracy" because it concentrates power and leaves no room for opposition except through revolution. Professor Berger agrees. They are both mistaken. Socialism too represents some democratic possibilities, possibilities that are complementary to those associated with the capitalist system. To grasp this, we need to remember the dialectical unity of capitalism and socialism. Socialism as a historic movement started as an emancipatory project generated not by writers and intellectuals, but by the oppressive excesses of capitalism itself. The great critique of capitalism is not *Das Kapital*, but the blue books of the nineteenth-century British factory inspectors. The socialist movement was saying that there is no freedom in Hobbism; that gross inequalities annul the rights and liberties of the lowly; and that we can improve the prospects for freedom and self-realization for all by pooling our resources, taking from each according to his abilities and giving to each according to her needs. However misguided the practice of "actually existing socialism" may have turned out to be in the end, these are ideas of great merit that opened new democratic vistas. Thus while socialism was not without grave problems, we cannot deny that the challenge it offered helped to render capitalism more progressive, and in doing so may well have saved it.

In keeping with his belief that all the ideas that ever legitimized socialism anywhere have been discredited, Berger attacks the notion of democratic socialism. Socialism and capitalism, he contends, are "two alternative modern systems of production"; there is no third way, but "only different versions and modifications of the two alternative models." He argues that Marx too treated the two systems as stark alternatives, and that the idea of social democracy rests on a confusion of the sphere of production with that of distribution.

In fact, Marx makes a strict distinction between socialism and capitalism only to override it. His argument was precisely that the distinction between the two systems had disappeared, not trivially in the sphere of distribution but crucially in the sphere of production, yet without changing the distribution of the rewards in a more "social" (i.e., egalitarian) direction. That was the so-called contradiction between the socialization of production and the privatization of appropriation.

At any rate, it is now rather late in the day to be disputing over these issues. The owl of Minerva has already taken flight. Practically every country in the West, including the United States, is for all practical purposes a social democracy—and for good reasons. They all have the good sense to recognize that social Darwinism has to be restrained as much as state power, that we simply cannot dispense with the notion of society as a commonwealth of persons with common concerns.

There are disturbing intimations of "developmentalism" in these essays. In accord with conventional wisdom, they implicitly hegemonize economic growth. Capitalism bests socialism economically because it is more conducive to economic growth. Capitalism bests socialism politically by being more conducive to democracy, but it engenders democracy by fostering economic growth. In both cases, economic growth is the decisive value. It is all too easy from here to slide into developmentalism and reconcile ourselves to all manner of repressive regimes, so long as they can plausibly claim to be pursuing economic growth. There are even whiffs of the notion that democracy is less than desirable for countries bracing for economic takeoff. In this spirit, every Third World autocrat enforces silence and conformity in the name of development, which eventually is supposed to make everyone better off. Would Stalinism be acceptable if it were more productive? I do not know how social scientists such as Berger and Kim would answer this question, but I do know how a democrat ought to answer it.

Finally, I think we must go beyond discursive strategies that define whole regions of the globe as beyond the pale of democratization. If we reduce democracy to liberal democracy and insist that only affluent capitalist societies can be democratic, democracy becomes irrelevant to a large part of the world. But there is no part of the world where democracy is not relevant, if only as an emancipatory project. There is no undemocratic country I know of where democratic struggles are not being waged. How do we explain these struggles? More to the point, what stance should we take toward them? Ought we to pretend that they are nonexistent or irrelevant, as our authors' theories might suggest? As far as I am concerned, that stance is not responsible because it will not help those who are justly waging struggles against violent autocrats on the rampage in Africa.

One final word about Schumpeter. I used to be skeptical about his conclusions. Yet as I have watched the current triumphalism of the West and analyzed the modes of thought and action that are associated with it, I have come increasingly to suspect that Schumpeter may have been right when he claimed that the real problem for capitalism is not its failures or its opponents, but its success. The prevailing atmosphere in the West today reminds me very much of the *respublica christiana* just before the Reformation.

4.
DEMOCRACY AND DEVELOPMENT

Jagdish Bhagwati

Jagdish Bhagwati *is the Arthur Lehman Professor of Economics and professor of political science at Columbia University. He is also economic policy advisor to the director general of the General Agreement on Tariffs and Trade (GATT). He has published several scientific papers and is the author and editor of over 30 books, including* Protectionism *(1988), which has been translated into several languages. His latest book,* The World Trading System at Risk *(1991), is now in its second printing and has been published in Japanese translation. He writes frequently for the* New York Times, *the* Wall Street Journal, *and the* Financial Times, *and is the recipient of several honorary doctorates, prizes, and other awards.*

It is ironic that Joseph Schumpeter, who was brought to Harvard's economics department largely on the basis of mathematical prowess that promised work more in the line of Léon Walras than Alfred Marshall, is today remembered for his broader and more sociological writings. It is equally ironic that, even as we have come to celebrate him, it is for the profound questions that he raised about the links among socialism, capitalism, and democracy rather than for his answers, which have lost their cogency.

Yet perhaps this is not so odd, for we economists often judge the significance of our colleagues and predecessors more by the questions they ask than by the answers they give. Why Schumpeter erred in his predictions, anticipating as he did the triumph of socialism, is itself a question of considerable interest. The answer may lie in his psyche, now illuminated by the new works on his life by Richard Swedberg.[1] Commenting on these, economist Paul Samuelson recently remarked:

> My guess that the 52-year-old Schumpeter I first met in 1935, for all his gaiety and bravado, was a sad person is more than confirmed; indeed the diaries reveal him to have been a seriously depressed personality under the

surface. And although he made no bones about his conservatism in politics, I don't think that any of us realized quite how conservative he really was at heart. . . . Schumpeter went along with the popular belief that the mass of people are led by wishful thinking into expecting to happen what they want to happen. But as I have noticed in life, among sophisticated people like Schumpeter, all goes into reverse: what they should hate to have happen, they paranoidly expect to happen.[2]

Interestingly, Schumpeter's pessimism was based, not on his economic analysis of the dynamics of capitalism—which he understood thoroughly and described brilliantly—but on a sociological analysis that focused on the presumed manner in which successful capitalism systematically undermines the precapitalist traditions that sustain it.

It was not Schumpeter but Friedrich Hayek who spotted the flaws in the reasoning of those, like Polish economist Oskar Lange, who claimed that socialism (with its central planning) would dominate capitalism because it would better calculate optimal prices. In advancing the then novel views that information is an essential input in the functioning of an economic system and that bureaucracies cannot compete with decentralized markets on this front, Hayek put his finger on the source of inefficiency under socialism.[3]

Bertrand Russell was thinking along similar lines when he predicted the problems that undemocratic socialism would create for individual initiative and scientific innovation. Focusing on what socialism would do to the former, he advised his readers:

Read Plato's *Republic* and More's *Utopia*—both socialist works—and imagine yourself living in the community portrayed by either. You will see that boredom would drive you to suicide or rebellion. . . . The impulse to danger and adventure is deeply ingrained in human nature, and no society which ignores it can long be stable. . . .[4]

On the topic of democracy and innovation, Russell had this to say:

Given two countries with equal natural resources, one a dictatorship and the other one allowing individual liberty, the one allowing liberty is almost certain to become superior to the other in war technique in no very long time. As we have seen in Germany and Russia, freedom in scientific research is incompatible with dictatorship. Germany might well have won the war if Hitler could have endured Jewish physicists. Russia will have less grain than if Stalin had not insisted upon the adoption of Lysenko's theories. It is highly probable that there will be, in Russia, a similar governmental incursion into the domain of nuclear physics. I do not doubt that, if there is no war during the next fifteen years, Russian scientific war technique will, at the end of that time, be very markedly inferior to that of the West, and that the inferiority will be directly traceable to dictatorship. I think, therefore, that, so long as powerful democracies exist, democracy in the long run will be victorious. And on this basis I allow myself a moderate optimism as to the future. Scientific dictatorships will perish through not being sufficiently scientific.[5]

Like most economists of his time, Hayek equated socialism with central planning, and he went on to warn of its inefficiency and potential for totalitarianism. Russell argued for democracy and outlined the ways in which socialism and totalitarianism would stifle human creativity and thus rob their own future. Their arguments were fine as far as they went, but it is hard to find great clarity in the way in which they thought of capitalism, socialism, and democracy or of the relationships among them.

Definitions and Linkages

These ambiguities of definition and linkage have continued into our time. The collapse of socialism behind the Iron Curtain was in equal parts the collapse of central planning and of totalitarianism. Yet the triumph (at least for now) of capitalism is not necessarily the triumph of *laissez-faire* or of democracy. In analyzing what history, both recent and not so recent, has taught us about the links among capitalism, socialism, and democracy, it is necessary to be certain what precisely we mean by these terms, which seem so obvious and yet are so obscure. Consider first the concepts themselves.

Socialism versus "market economies" or "capitalism." By socialism, I mean the *public ownership of the means of production* and the corresponding *exercise of control* by the public sector. I add the latter proviso since it is perfectly possible for the state to own productive means but leave their management in private hands (as Swedish and Indian intellectuals have sometimes recommended), or for the private sector to own property whose day-to-day use the state controls (as may happen during the course of the privatization process in Eastern Europe). The regimes that once held sway in Eastern Europe and the former Soviet Union were fully socialist by this definition, leaving little space for (legal) private ownership and hence denying altogether the possibility of pluralistic economic activity.

Such exemplars of the centrally planned economy stand at one extreme of a continuum that spans varying degrees of public ownership and control. The other extreme—complete *laissez-faire*—remains elusive: after all, governments get elected or seize power to do things, not to self-destruct à la Bakunin or Milton Friedman.

The definition of socialism in terms of production rather than distribution is consonant with Marx. However uneasy it may make economists who wish closely to couple production and distribution, empirical evidence does not show any tight linkages between productive relations and distributive aspirations or outcomes.

Peter Berger is thus eminently sensible in embracing the production-related definition of socialism. "Market economy" or "capitalism" is defined equally by the private ownership of the means of production and the associated exercise of private management.

Democracy versus totalitarianism. The definition of democracy is no less a problem. It is perhaps easy to define it by what it is not: totalitarian states are readily identified. But as Kyung-won Kim notes, democracy may be absent even when it is professed. (I am not referring here, of course, to the obvious travesty of totalitarian dictatorships professing to be "people's democracies.")

Schumpeter thought of democracy as a process; Kyung-won Kim wants to take outcomes into account as well. The absence of a spirit of toleration, the tyranny of the majority, the uncompromising rule of the party that gets first past the post in elections—none of these is consonant with the spirit of democracy. Concern with "rights" leavens the democratic process in ways that might be ignored by those wedded to a purely "utilitarian" view of governance. Once again, however, we must deal with a continuum on several dimensions, and also with judgments that we may find it hard to get others to share.

The concepts "democracy," "socialism," and "capitalism," then, may be defined with a fair amount of clarity but still lack sufficient precision to allow us always to file countries and experiences neatly into one box or another. Nonetheless, the questions that Berger and Kim address concerning the linkages among democracy, socialism, and capitalism do admit of plausible answers.

I shall concentrate on two of these questions: 1) Does democracy require a market economy? and 2) Can a market economy exist when democracy does not?

As for the first question, I entirely agree with Berger's view that democracy does require a market economy. Empirical evidence to date shows no example of a democracy that is or was fully socialist (i.e., that had no private ownership of the means of production).

I suspect that the reason must lie in the possibility of political dissent, without which democracy is impossible. Dissent cannot be altogether stamped out even by draconian regimes. But it takes heroes to dissent when the cost of doing so is immense, whereas democracy flourishes only when average men and women can voice their dissatisfaction. The cost of dissent is immense when those who hold political authority also control the means of production: keeping one's job and even sheer economic survival then requires political circumspection and conformity.

With respect to the second question, I would again answer in the affirmative: a market economy can exist in the absence of democracy. The answers to our two questions, then, add up to the conclusion that a market economy is a necessary, but not a sufficient, condition for democracy.

Empirical evidence again underlines this strongly. Berger and Kim remind us of recent models of successful market-economy development under essentially undemocratic regimes in East Asia. Ralf Dahrendorf's analysis of German history (which Kim cites) also confirms this.[6]

It is possible, however, to reconcile this with the view, associated with Barrington Moore's classic work, that the rise of the bourgeoisie resulted in democracy.[7] Both Berger and Kim provide the ground for this reconciliation by citing what I call the probable *long-term incompatibility* of a successful market economy with lack of democracy. The autonomous spheres of economic action that a market economy inevitably creates will, *in the presence of successful modernization or economic development*, create an assertive middle class that will seek the political freedoms that democracy provides.[8] This appears to be the recent experience of the undemocratic regimes in East Asia, where the growth of successful market economies has led to rising demands for political freedoms and self-government.

Today, this process receives tremendous added impetus from the information revolution, which spreads not merely the ideology of consumerism, but the culture of democracy. Democracy has also become increasingly understood as an integral component of human rights, providing the external countervailing power to internal authoritarianism. Finally, I suspect that in the case of East Asia's "little dragons" the direct role played by extremely high literacy rates in both economic development and the growth of political demands for democracy must not be ignored.

In addition to the pair of questions discussed above, at least two others remain of interest today. Schumpeter's gloomy forecast of capitalism's collapse has certainly failed to come true, but can a similar pessimism about the future of democracy be ruled out of court? While democracy has certainly triumphed for the moment, Peter Berger is absolutely right in suggesting that triumphalism is unwarranted. History itself suggests that there is no "end of history." The pendulum swings and swings again. It is necessary therefore to return to the old question that we wrestled with in the 1950s: is democracy sustainable if it will (even temporarily) *discourage* economic development? Failure to generate growing incomes in developing countries would certainly threaten to undermine democracy by fostering or exacerbating harsh and divisive conditions of zero-sum social conflict.

The other question has to do with transitions to democracy and markets by the erstwhile socialists of Eastern Europe and the former Soviet Union. In what sequence should *perestroika* and *glasnost'* be arranged for a successful transition; in other words, should democracy precede or follow a market economy? Who was right, Gorbachev or Deng Xiaoping?

A New Look at the "Cruel Choice"

As reflection on development strategies for newly decolonized countries began in earnest in the 1950s, there was considerable skepticism about the ability of democracies to compete in the race against totalitarian regimes. In fact, it seemed evident that democratic ideas and countries were fated to suffer a disadvantage in this contest. To understand why, it is necessary to recollect the mind-set at the root of the conception of development that then prevailed.

The Harrod-Domar model, much used then, analyzed development in terms of two parameters: the rate of investment and the productivity of capital. For policy-making purposes, the latter was largely treated as "given," so debate centered on the question of how to promote investment. This approach favored by mainstream economists coincided with the Marxist focus on "primitive accumulation" as the mainspring of industrialization and also with the cumbersome quasi-Marxist models elaborated in the investment-allocation literature that grew up around Maurice Dobb.

But if the focus was on accumulation, with productivity considered a datum, it was evident that democracies would be handicapped vis-à-vis totalitarian regimes. Writing in the mid-1960s, I noted "the cruel choice between rapid (self-sustained) expansion and democratic processes."[9] This view, which political scientist Atul Kohli has christened the "cruel choice" thesis, was widely shared by economists at the time.[10] Later emphasis would shift away from raising the rate of savings and investment (dimensions on which most developing countries did well) to getting the most for one's blood, sweat, and tears (dimensions on which developing countries performed in diverse ways). Indeed, by the 1980s it was manifest that the policy framework determining the productivity of investment was absolutely critical, and that winners and losers would be sorted out by the choices they made in this regard. Democracy then no longer looked so bad: it could provide better incentives, relate development to people, and offset any accumulationist disadvantage that it might produce.

Indeed, as Kohli has emphasized, the growth rates of democracies have not been noticeably worse than those of undemocratic regimes.[11] I also disagree with the common view that the undemocratic nature of the regimes in South Korea, Taiwan, Singapore, and Hong Kong was the key to their phenomenal growth. This is a *non sequitur*, a choice example of the *post hoc ergo propter hoc* fallacy. These regimes owe their phenomenal success to their rapid transition to an export-oriented trade strategy (which first enabled them to profit from the unprecedented growth in the world economy through the 1960s, and then positioned them to continue as major competitors in world markets), as well as to their high rates of literacy (which economists now generally acknowledge to be an important "producer good"). Both of these growth-promoters were present in part because of the geographic proximity of Japan and the power of its example.

Similarly, India's failures in both these areas, which help to explain its relatively poor development performance, can be blamed in large part on the intellectual affinity that its governing classes harbored for both Fabian politics and Cambridge economics.[12] Neither East Asian authoritarianism nor Indian democracy explains, in my view, the differences in their levels of economic performance. Democrats have little to fear, and even less to learn, from the East Asian experience with authoritarian regimes, at least as far as economic development is concerned.

Sequencing and the Road from Socialism

Considerably greater ambiguity, however, surrounds the other urgent issue today: the correct sequencing of the introduction of democracy and of capitalism (or market reforms) in the great escape from socialism-cum-totalitarianism. Gorbachev's choice in the Soviet Union (assuming he had an ultimate transition to capitalism in mind) was to push for *glasnost'* more rapidly than *perestroika*. Deng Xiaoping (assuming he had an ultimate transition to democracy in mind) chose the opposite sequence.

At first glance, the Gorbachev sequence seemed sensible. The appetite for political freedom could be immediately satiated. Economic reforms, on the other hand, would inevitably take time, and the residue of satisfaction left over from political reforms might provide a breathing space in which to implement economic reforms.[13]

As it happened, the politics got increasingly more complex as the Baltic states grew more restive, other republics began to assert themselves against the center, and Gorbachev became locked in a power struggle with Boris Yeltsin. These political conflicts tore the economy apart as the USSR went from stalled microeconomic reforms to macroeconomic crisis. The coup of 1991 brought Yeltsin to power; now the economy is virtually under the tutelage of the G-7, and a former superpower has been reduced to the role of a superbeggar in the aid game.

By contrast, the Chinese approach chalked up considerable economic success; this very success, however, unleashed political forces that, ill-managed, led to the tragedy of Tiananmen Square and temporary reverses in economic reforms. Nonetheless, China's path, unlike that of the former Soviet Union, so far seems fairly stable; it has also saved China from falling to the abject level at which the economically devastated Commonwealth of Independent States currently finds itself.

The jury is still out, however, on the question of sequencing—one has to be able to separate out the features peculiar to the Soviet case that contributed to the failure of the sequence chosen by Gorbachev. The contrasting choices of Gorbachev and Deng Xiaoping and their respective fates will continue to provide a fascinating intellectual puzzle for students of capitalism, socialism, and democracy as the transition away from undemocratic socialism unfolds in the coming decade.

NOTES

1. Richard Swedberg, *Schumpeter: A Biography* (Princeton: Princeton University Press, 1991) and idem, ed., *Joseph A. Schumpeter: The Economics and Sociology of Capitalism* (Princeton: Princeton University Press, 1991).

2. Paul A. Samuelson, "Homage to Chakravarty: Thoughts on His Lumping Schumpeter with Marx to Define a Paradigm Alternative to Mainstream Growth Theories" (unpublished manuscript, Massachusetts Institute of Technology, August 1991).

3. Friedrich Hayek, *Knowledge, Evolution, and Society* (London: Butler and Tanner, 1983).

4. Bertrand Russell, *The Impact of Science on Society* (New York: Simon and Schuster, 1953), 68-69.

5. Ibid., 54-55.

6. See Ralf Dahrendorf, *Society and Democracy in Germany* (New York: Doubleday, 1969).

7. Cf. Barrington Moore, *Social Origins of Dictatorship and Democracy* (Boston: Beacon Press, 1966).

8. Equally, unsuccessful economic development could imperil the survival of democracy. Whether democracy will encourage or discourage economic development is therefore a critical issue. (I consider it at p. 42 above.)

9. Jagdish Bhagwati, *The Economics of Underdeveloped Countries* (London and New York: Weidenfeld and Nicholson and McGraw Hill, 1966), 204.

10. Cf. Atul Kohli, "Democracy and Development," in John P. Lewis and Valeriana Kallab, eds., *Development Strategies Reconsidered* (Washington, D.C.: Overseas Development Council, 1986), 156.

11. Ibid.

12. Myron Weiner's *The Child and the State in India: Child Labor and Educational Policy in Comparative Perspective* (Princeton: Princeton University Press, 1991) offers an excellent analysis of the endogenous social and cultural reasons for India's neglect of primary education and its failure to reduce illiteracy.

13. This viewpoint is cogently argued in Padma Desai, *Perestroika in Perspective* (Princeton: Princeton University Press, 1989), which compares and contrasts the Soviet with the Chinese sequencing strategies.

5.
THE NEOLIBERAL FALLACY

Adam Przeworski

Adam Przeworski *is Martin A. Ryerson Distinguished Service Professor of Political Science and codirector of the Center for Rationality, Ethics, and Society at the University of Chicago. He received his M.A. from the University of Warsaw and his Ph.D. from Northwestern University. He has been a research associate at the Ecole Pratique des Hautes Etudes in Paris and a visiting professor at FLACSO in Santiago, Chile. His publications include* Capitalism and Social Democracy *(1985),* Democracy and the Market: Political and Economic Reforms in Eastern Europe and Latin America *(1991), and* Economic Reforms in New Democracies: A Social-Democratic Approach *(1992).*

Ours is an era of ideology. Several countries, in Eastern Europe and elsewhere, have recently begun the greatest ideologically inspired experiment since Josef Stalin initiated the forced industrialization of the Soviet Union in 1929. Although the prevailing mood echoes Konrad Adenauer's dictum of "no experiments," the economic transformations envisaged in these countries ironically mirror the communist project. They implement an intellectual blueprint, a blueprint drawn up within the walls of American academia and shaped by international financial institutions. These transformations are meant to have radical effects, to turn all existing social relations upside down. They offer a panacea, a magic elixir which, once taken, will cure all ills. Replace "nationalization of the means of production" with "private property" and "plan" with "market," and you can leave the structure of the ideology intact. Perhaps revolutions are shaped by the very systems against which they are directed.

Facing what are often the gravest economic crises in their history, countries all around the globe are told to plunge in and persevere. They are exhorted to plunge into reforms about which only one thing can be known with certainty: they will make most people worse off for some time to come. They are urged to short-circuit the democratic process by introducing reforms so swiftly that citizens will have no time to mobilize effectively against them. Even after the pains of reform have made themselves felt, politicians are urged to stay the course, which most do. Union leaders speak publicly of their "hope [that] there will be unemployment." Finance ministers declare that if unemployment fails to rise to 8 or 10 percent, it will be "a sign that the reforms are not working." Government leaders declare their determination to persist "regardless of all the political pressures upon us."[1]

Neoliberal ideology, emanating from the United States and various multinational agencies, claims that the choice is obvious: there is only one path to development, and it must be followed. Proponents of this ideology argue as if they had a Last Judgment picture of the world, a general model of economic and political dynamics that allows them to assess the ultimate consequences of all partial steps.[2]

Yet this model is no more than a mixture of evidence, argument from first principles, self-interest, and wishful thinking. Moreover, even though market ideology now seems to have attained uncontested intellectual hegemony, the virtues of markets are being called strongly into question by recent developments in neoclassical economic theory—the very body of thought that heretofore has underpinned the claim that markets are efficient allocators of resources. The observations that a complete set of markets is unfeasible, and that information is inevitably imperfect, invalidate the case for the efficiency of the invisible hand.[3] Moreover, observed patterns of economic growth cannot be explained without a recourse to externalities, thus thwarting any expectation that competitive markets are efficient in dynamic terms.[4]

Confronted with the real world, market ideology fares no better. The thematic statement for this symposium cites as the model to follow "the United States and other key countries in the West [that] have been governed for the past decade by conservative, pro-private enterprise parties." Yet if a Martian were asked to pick the most efficient and humane economic systems on earth, it would certainly not choose the countries that rely most on markets. The United States is a stagnant economy in which real wages have been constant for more than a decade and the real income of the poorer 40 percent of the population has declined. It is an inhumane society in which 11.5 percent of the population—some 28 million people, including 20 percent of all children—lives in poverty. It is the oldest democracy on earth, but has one of the lowest voter-participation rates in the democratic world, and the highest per capita prison population in the world. Is this the model to follow?

These remarks should not be construed as a defense of traditional patterns of state intervention, whether under capitalism or socialism; as an argument against relying on markets; or as an attack on promarket reforms. They are, rather, intended as parts of a cautionary tale warning against the dangers of excessive ideological zeal. What I argue below is that we still know little about markets and democracies, and that the little we do know does not support any ideological blueprints.

Markets and Efficiency

In the first moments of postcommunist euphoria in Eastern Europe, the model to follow seemed obvious. Yet vague notions about "moving in the direction of 'normal' economies," "embracing the model tested by the historical experience of the developed countries," or "constructing a market economy like in the West" were not, are not, and cannot be sufficient to guide the process of economic transformation. "Normal" economies differ greatly among themselves—in the degree of state intervention; in the way that their firms, industries, and financial institutions are organized; in their collective bargaining systems; and in their system of social welfare provision. Imitating the United States does not point in the same direction as imitating Sweden or Japan. Moreover, it is not at all certain that the alternatives facing Eastern Europe are indeed limited to those already tested elsewhere. For one thing, some kind of a reformed state sector is likely to continue producing most of the national product in these countries within the foreseeable future. In addition, sentiment for some kind of a workers' self-management system remains strong.

In broad outline, the issues are: the role of the state in coordinating resource allocation, the welfare and distributional properties of alternative structures of ownership, and development strategies, if any. The long history of reflection on these problems need not concern us here. Instead, I will focus solely on questions that are of immediate practical significance in the global East and South.

Those who expect the market to coordinate economic activities to produce intertemporally efficient allocations of resources assume the truth of the proposition—known as the first theorem of welfare economics—that competitive markets are sufficient to generate efficiency, at least in the absence of public goods, externalities, or increasing returns. Yet this belief has been undermined by the development of the economics of incomplete markets and imperfect information. As Joseph Stiglitz puts it, "Adam Smith's invisible hand may be more like the Emperor's new clothes: invisible because it is not there."[5]

The blueprint of efficient markets was developed gradually by late nineteenth- and early twentieth-century economists like Léon Walras and Vilfredo Pareto before being formalized by Kenneth Arrow and Georges Debreu in 1954.[6] The model is simple: Individuals know that they have needs and endowments, and they freely produce and exchange goods and services. In equilibrium, all individuals' expectations are fulfilled, and all markets clear. Hence the prices at which individuals exchange reflect their preferences and the relative scarcities of various goods and services; these prices inform individuals about all the opportunities they forsake. As a result, resources are allocated in such a way that all gains from trade are exhausted; no one can be better off without someone else being worse off; and the resulting distribution of welfare would not be altered under a unanimity rule. These are three equivalent definitions of collective rationality (also known as Pareto optimality).

The case for markets as efficient resource allocators hinges on the assumption that markets are "complete," or in other words, that there is a "market" for every contingent state of nature. But as Kenneth Arrow himself showed in 1964, this assumption is unwarranted: some futures markets, particularly risk markets, are inevitably missing.[7] With some markets absent, prices no longer summarize all the opportunity costs, which implies that not all economic agents are operating with the same information. Labor markets, capital markets, and goods markets do not clear, and the resulting allocation will have room for improvement. Moreover, as Greenwald and Stiglitz have shown, if any markets are missing, then even the allocation of those resources for which markets do exist will not be efficient.[8]

To examine the effect of market-oriented reforms on growth, we need to distinguish three questions: 1) Why do stabilization and liberalization (of foreign trade and domestic competition) induce recessions? 2) Why do some stabilization programs undermine future growth? 3) Are stability and competition sufficient for a resumption of growth?[9]

Stabilization programs tend to induce recessions, even when they are not accompanied by liberalization. There are at least two reasons for this: stabilization is usually achieved by reducing demand; and successful stabilization makes interest rates soar. Moreover, the reduction or elimination of subsidies to industries, price supports, and import tariffs, along with domestic antimonopoly measures, all tend to depress rates of return on investment and boost unemployment.

While high interest rates may be transitory, their effects linger after the initial period of stabilization is over. As Stanley Fischer has pointed out:

> Investment will not resume until real interest rates reach a reasonable level, and prolonged periods of high real interest rates create financial crises and bankruptcies even for firms that would be viable at reasonable levels of interest rate.[10]

The second reason why stabilization programs often undermine the prospects for future growth has been highlighted by Vito Tanzi, who observed that spending cuts made under the pressure of fiscal crises tend not to discriminate between government consumption and public investment. After examining several instances in which stabilization policies undermined the capacity for growth, Tanzi concluded:

In all these examples, the *supply* has been reduced, thus creating imbalances that, in time, have manifested themselves as excessive demand. In these cases, demand-management policies alone would have reduced the symptoms of these imbalances but would not have eliminated the causes. Thus, stabilization programs might succeed stabilization programs without bringing about a durable adjustment.[11]

Indeed, investment projects are often politically easier to cut than government services or public employment. Both public investments in infrastructure and measures to induce private investment are reduced, thus diminishing future supply.

Finally, even if they are successful in their own terms, market-oriented reforms are not likely to generate conditions conducive to growth. Neoclassical economic theory had little to say about growth. Its preoccupations were mainly static, and anyone who has read Schumpeter knows that static efficiency is a poor criterion of welfare. Dynamic economies are not efficient in the static sense: they use a number of techniques, with different cost-benefit ratios. In turn, the question of whether a competitive market generates dynamic efficiency is highly complex. The theory that did emerge from neoclassical economics, the Solow-Swan model of exogenous growth, argued that competitive equilibrium is efficient but also that it leads to stagnation of income in the absence of exogenous population growth and exogenous technical change. This theory predicted that the levels of economic development should converge among all countries, and they do not.[12] Recent models do provide an endogenous explanation of economic growth, but in these theories the competitive equilibrium is no longer efficient.[13] The "engine of growth" is a set of externalities in education, skills, technology, and so on. Competitive markets, in which firms do not capture full return to their endowments, tend to undersupply the factors that generate such externalities.

The State and Economic Growth

Hence the present state of economic theory does not support the conclusion that competitive markets are sufficient either to allocate resources efficiently or to generate growth. Whether one takes the theory of incomplete markets, with their informational asymmetries; or the theory of endogenous growth, with constant returns to a single factor and externalities; or the theory of non-Walrasian trade, one will discover neoclassical arguments which suggest that some state intervention is necessary for growth. The notion that the market by itself can efficiently allocate scarce resources is purely hortatory.[14]

The central lesson of the endogenous-growth theories is the importance of education, whether measured by school-enrollment rates or by indices such as literacy. Primary education for women has particularly high returns in terms of per capita growth. And while no similar statistical studies seem to be available with regard to health expenditures, the World Bank's 1991 *World Development Report* cites impressive evidence on the productivity-boosting effects of health programs, as well as the strong statistical correlation between more equal distributions of income and faster growth.

The effect of public investment on growth is a topic too controversial to be dealt with in a summary fashion, yet recent research summarized by Gene Grossman shows that governments should engage in infrastructural investments not supplied efficiently by private agents, and should pursue measures that increase the rate of return to private projects.[15] This role includes a selective industrial policy that would comprise preferential credit rates for high-technology industries (in which the market rate of return is much lower than the social rate); for projects that suffer from high costs of entry, substantial economies of scale, or steep learning curves; and for projects that have potential spillovers across firms due to externalities and asymmetries of information between buyers and producers. Other recent findings by economists such as Robert Barro and Ronald Findlay reinforce the idea that some intermediate level of public investment and employment—far below 100 percent but also far above zero—is optimal for economic growth.[16]

These findings concerning the role of the state in promoting and sustaining development raise the fundamental institutional question of how to organize state institutions so that they intervene only when appropriate. Neoliberal economists such as Robert Tollison and George Stigler remind us that the state's ability to engage in productive activities or differentially favor private projects can easily give rise to rent seeking.[17] But while the question of the socially optimal institutional rules and structures remains open, it would be a mistake to answer that the state should be prevented from any discretionary intervention, limiting its role to promoting the "freedom of individual enterprise." Problems of institutional design cannot be solved by pretending that the state can somehow be walled off from the economy, but must be confronted as such.

Nor can institutional questions be limited to the role of "the state." Any capitalist economy, in which markets are inevitably incomplete and particular economic agents have access to different information, includes several different types of principals and agents: managers and employees, owners and managers, creditors and entrepreneurs, citizens and politicians. The performance of particular firms—and ultimately of the whole economy—depends on the design of institutions that regulate these relations. What matters is whether the employees have incentives and can be monitored to maximize effort; whether managers have incentives and can be monitored to maximize profits; and whether the state has incentives and can be monitored to resist pressure from weak firms or special interests. To speak of "the market" as the object of "state intervention" obscures the real issues: the problem we face is not a simple matter of "the market" versus "the state," but of specific institutional mechanisms that can provide particular economic agents, including the state, with incentives and information that will lead them to behave in a collectively rational manner.[18]

The practical consequences of ignoring such issues are best illustrated by the vagaries of privatization in Eastern Europe. Former Polish finance minister Leszek Balcerowicz has defended privatization as follows:

> A market economy based on a broad participation of different forms of private ownership permits the achievement of the highest degree of effectiveness—among all economic systems known in practice—in using the material and spiritual resources of a society. As a result, it generates the quickest improvement in the living standard of citizens. This is so because economizing costs, good organization of work, high quality of production, the effective search for new markets, and technical progress and development are in the interest of *the proprietors who direct the work of enterprises.*[19]

These kinds of hopes regarding privatization rest on three false assumptions: 1) that private property will solve principal-agent problems, forcing managers to maximize profit; 2) that the market is a source of incentives for employees rather than information for managers; and 3) that enough capital will be forthcoming to infuse investment into newly private firms. The first two assumptions are based on nineteenth-century conceptions of capitalism. To see the flaw in the last assumption requires only elementary accounting: given that private savings in Eastern Europe do not exceed 10 percent of capital stock, and assuming that foreigners will buy at most another 10 percent, where is the rest of the capital to come from? As a result of such misconceptions, Poland has spent two years arguing about privatization, leaving in uncertainty the status of the state enterprises that continue to produce about 70 percent of nonagricultural output.

Democracy and Economic Performance

One would certainly wish to agree with the Bonn Conference on Economic Cooperation in Europe that "democratic institutions and economic freedom foster economic and social progress." Yet given the current state of knowledge, we do not know if this is true. The underlying premise is that democracy safeguards property rights and these in turn, by diminishing the risk to investors, foster economic growth. It may be true, as some have argued, that secure property rights foster growth. Yet, even if democracy fosters growth, it must be for reasons other than its guarantee of property rights. Moreover, we do not know whether democracy promotes economic development, hinders it, or is irrelevant to it.

The statistical evidence is inconclusive and the studies that produced it are all seriously flawed. I reviewed 17 studies that generated 20 findings (some distinguished separate areas or periods).[20] Among them, eight found in favor of democracy and eight in favor of authoritarianism; the other four discovered no difference. What is even more puzzling is that among the 11 results published in 1987 or earlier, eight found that authoritarian regimes grew faster, while none of the nine results published after 1987 supported this finding. Since this difference does not seem attributable to samples or periods, one can only wonder about the relation between statistics and ideology. Due to certain technical problems, I hesitate to attach much significance to these results one way or another. Hence I am not suggesting that democracy generates inferior economic performance—only that we still do not know what the facts are.

Democracy may promote economic growth for a variety of reasons: for example, because it is informationally efficient in the sense of punishing bad rulers and rewarding good ones.[21] But democracy as such does not necessarily safeguard property rights.

The market is a system in which scarce resources are allocated to alternative uses by decentralized decisions. Yet under capitalism property is institutionally distinct from authority: individuals are simultaneously market agents and citizens. As a result, there are two mechanisms by which resources can be allocated to uses and distributed among households—the market and the state. The market is a mechanism in which individuals cast "votes" for allocations with the resources they own, resources that are always distributed unequally; the state is a system that allocates resources which it does not own, with rights distributed differently from the market. Hence the two mechanisms lead to the same outcome only by a fluke. The allocation of resources that individuals prefer as citizens generally fails to coincide with the allocation that they decide upon through the market.

Democracy's rule of "one citizen, one vote" exacerbates this divergence by equalizing the right to influence the allocation of resources through the state. It is hardly surprising that distributions of consumption produced by the market differ from those collectively preferred by the electorate, since democracy offers those who are poor, oppressed, or otherwise dissatisfied with the initial distribution of endowments an opportunity to seek redress via the state. Endowed with political power in the form of universal suffrage, those who suffer as a consequence of private property will attempt to use this power to redistribute wealth. To put it in technical terms: if the median voter is decisive, and if the market-generated distribution of income is skewed toward lower incomes (as it always is), then majority rule will call for an equality of incomes.[22]

The question of democracy's impact upon the institution of private property lay at the heart of debates over the rights to vote and to associate in Western Europe and North America during the nineteenth century. Conservatives concurred with socialists that democracy—specifically universal suffrage and the right of workers to organize—must threaten property. Madison, Macaulay, Ricardo, and Marx all agreed that people with little or no property would use their political rights to expropriate those with more, thus undermining capitalism. The Scottish philosopher James Mackintosh predicted in 1818 that if the "laborious classes" were to gain the franchise, "a permanent animosity between opinion and property must be the consequence." David Ricardo was prepared to extend suffrage only "to that part of [the people] which cannot be supposed to have an interest in overturning the right to property."[23] Thomas Babington Macaulay, in his 1842 speech on the Chartists, pictured universal suffrage as the end of property and thus of all civilization.[24] Eight years later, Karl Marx expressed the same conviction that private property and universal suffrage are incompatible.[25]

> "...society, by which I mean all the people of a country acting through a democratic process, can decide collectively that goods other than those maximized by the market should be the goal of development."

In retrospect, these conclusions were obviously too strong. There are 14 countries in the world today that have remained continuously capitalist and democratic for the past half-century. Yet if "the people" (in its eighteenth-century singular) is sovereign, it may prefer an allocation and distribution of resources that differs from the market outcome. To cite Brian Barry, "It is precisely because the market is incompatible with the introduction of considerations of distributive justice that it cannot be accepted as the arbiter of income distribution." As Diane Elson has nicely put it, in the market, "choice in the small does not provide choice in the large"; individuals can choose but society cannot.[26] And society, by which I mean all the people of a country acting through a democratic process, can decide collectively that goods other than those maximized by the market should be the goal of development. Democracy inevitably threatens "property rights."

Yet democracies are not all the same. Systems of representation, arrangements for dividing and supervising power, methods of organizing interests, legal doctrines, and the rights and obligations associated with citizenship differ significantly across regimes in which parties compete and individuals enjoy political rights. Taken together, such differences generate effects which, in spite of two thousand years of reflection and investigation, are still poorly understood.

More specifically, we need to know the conditions under which democratic institutions work and endure. By "work," I mean that they achieve such widely desired effects as economic growth, material security, freedom from arbitrary violence, and so on. By "endure," I mean that they absorb and effectively regulate all major conflicts, so that laws and other rules are changed only in a lawful and regular fashion. Odd as it may seem, the answers elude us even today.

This is not to say that there are no clues—studies of developed capitalist countries, for instance, show that until the early 1980s, better economic performance was most often enjoyed by countries in which encompassing, centralized unions negotiated with employers in the presence of a state controlled by a social democratic party. Statistical analyses of the OECD countries have shown repeatedly that lower income inequality, more extensive welfare services, a more favorable trade-off between employment and inflation, a more favorable trade-off between wages and investment, and a more favorable trade-off between growth and social policies are to be found in countries that combine strong unions with social democratic control over the government.

My own study of 14 OECD countries between 1960 and 1981 shows that the welfare of the average adult, the average worker, and the average manufacturing employee was higher in social democratic countries. (Welfare here is defined as the utility, taking into account risk aversion, of a lottery composed of market income, unemployment compensation, and social wage.) To put it simply, the only countries in the world in which almost no one is poor after taxes and transfers are those that pursue social democratic policies.[27]

What seems to matter for economic performance and social welfare, then, is not just "democracy" in general but specific democratic institutions and policies. Indeed, the correct question is not whether democracy as we have known it will develop in the countries that have recently experienced a collapse of authoritarianism, but rather which sorts of democratic institutions, and with what economic outcomes, are likely to emerge.

Modernization via Internationalization?

While the causes of the collapse of growth in the global South and East are hard to diagnose, the most common response to it seems easier to identify. It is best described as "modernization via internationalization." Different political forces in the capitalist South and the postcommunist East see no alternative but to embark on the "North-West Passage"—a road that would lead their societies to the "First World," for some "the North," for others "the West." This is a strategy of trying to adopt the political, economic, and cultural patterns (democracy, markets, and consumerist individualism) that dominate the advanced capitalist world. Modernization becomes synonymous with internationalization.

The political and economic program that guides the most important political forces throughout Eastern Europe is to "join the West" or "reenter Europe." This program is based on what we might call "the East European syllogism." The major premise of this syllogism is, "If it had not been for communism, we would be like the West." The minor premise is "Now communism is gone." The conclusion not only asserts that Eastern Europe should and will embrace the Western model, but also promises that this model will generate the wealth and glamor of developed capitalism. Similar notions are current in Latin America, as witness Mexican president Carlos Salinas de Gortari's promise to take his country to "the First World," or Brazilian president Fernando Collor de Mello's talk of *integracão competitiva*.

This strategy appears to be without precedent in history. All previous attempts at modernization conceived of development as a project linked to national, economic, and political independence. All previous modernizing leaders asserted the importance of national cultures, called for political institutions consistent with national traditions, and envisaged growth led by national industries and oriented toward local markets.[28] In contrast, the strategy of modernization by internationalization explicitly accepts at least a partial surrender of national sovereignty in the political, economic, and cultural realms. This strategy opens local markets to foreign penetration, abolishes cultural barriers, and seeks to model political institutions on patterns developed elsewhere. Coca-Cola is no longer the imperialist drug but the nectar of universal prosperity.

History shows that even in those cases where modernization was a strategy of autonomous national development, it tended to create enormous tensions by bringing about changes in the distribution of income, shifts in power relations, and profound cultural transformations. Far from escaping such tensions, the pursuit of modernization via internationalization actually exacerbates them. There are two reasons for this. The first lies in the strategy's competitive nature: all countries cannot simultaneously have a positive balance of payments. The race to modernize will inevitably have its winners and losers. Moreover, the winners and the losers will not be nation-states but regions, sectors, industries, and particular social groups. Sharp increases in regional, sectoral, and social inequality across and within nations will follow. At the same time, this strategy requires national governments to relinquish some of the traditional instruments of economic policy: they peg exchange rates, they adjust demand to that of their trading partners, they subject themselves to various targets and conditions set by international lenders. As a result, national governments suffer a serious decline in their capacity to compensate losers and manage social tensions generally. Democracy suffers as well when decisions that were once controlled by elected national officials pass into the hands of actors who cannot be voted in or out. The combination of increasing inequality and decreasing national sovereignty threatens to exacerbate social conflicts and weaken nascent democratic institutions.

The policy style inherent in neoliberal economic reform programs contributes to this process in the following way. Since the neoliberal "cure" is a painful one, with significant social costs, reforms tend to be initiated from above and launched by surprise, independently of public opinion and without the participation of organized political forces. Reforms tend to be enacted by fiat, or railroaded through legislatures without any changes reflecting the divergence of interests and opinions. The political style of implementation tends toward rule by decree; governments seek to mobilize their supporters rather than accept the compromises that might result from public consultation. In the end, the society is taught that it can vote but not choose; legislatures are given the impression that they have no role to play in the elaboration of policy; nascent political parties, trade unions, and other organizations learn that their voices do not count. The autocratic character of such "Washington-style" reforms helps to undermine representative institutions, personalize politics, and engender a climate in which politics becomes either reduced to fixes, or else inflated into a search for redemption. Thus even when neoliberal reforms make economic sense, they weaken representative institutions. In Poland, the four institutions enjoying the greatest citizen confidence when the first postcommunist government came into office in 1989 were the two houses of parliament, the Mazowiecki government, and the Catholic Church. Eighteen months into the economic reforms, the three institutions that enjoyed the most confidence were the army, the police, and the Church, in that order.

> *"Since the neoliberal 'cure' is a painful one, with significant social costs, reforms tend to be initiated from above and launched by surprise, independently of public opinion and without the participation of organized political forces."*

It is sobering to note how often strategies of modernization have failed in the past. Joining the First World club of democracy and prosperity is no mean feat. Since World War II, only Greece, Japan, Portugal, and Spain have done it. South Korea and Taiwan may be on the threshold; certainly they are the models that everyone wants to imitate. Yet while such accomplishments are not impossible, they have been exceedingly rare.

Is this road to the First World the only alternative available to the less developed countries of the East and South? Is this strategy viable economically? Can it gain and keep local political support in the face of massive dislocations caused by economic transformation and its attendant social costs? What sorts of cultural forces, nationalistic or religious, is this strategy likely to unleash? Where is it likely to lead, economically and politically? What kind of an international order will it create? What will happen if and when these strategies fail to generate prosperity?

My argument throughout has been only that we must take such questions seriously. Freedom and material security are things that most people prize highly, but ideological zeal tends only to increase human suffering—and many of the currently fashionable policy prescriptions are based on nothing more than zeal. Every time I apply for a government research grant, I am required to sign a form declaring that I will not experiment on human subjects. I wish governments had to do the same.

NOTES

1. The first statement, by Barbara Labuda, a leader of Solidarity and parliamentary deputy, is quoted in Zbigniew Domaranczyk, *100 dni Mazowieckiego* (Warsaw: Wydawnictwo Andrzej Bonarski, 1990). The second is from Economics Minister Vladimir Dlouhy of the Czech and Slovak Federative Republic, quoted in the *Financial Times* (London), 6 February 1991; while the last is from Poland's former finance minister Leszek Balcerowicz, *Financial Times* (London), 16 July 1990.

2. This posture is puzzling given how flimsy is the knowledge on which this advice, and the money that follows the words, are based. As one reads the successive World Bank *Development Reports*, one finds solid research which speaks in favor of mobilizing public savings, supports the importance of income equality and of educational and health expenditures for economic growth, and highlights cautionary tales about the dangers of financial deregulation and badly timed trade liberalization. Yet the policy recommendations are as one in insisting on the virtues of markets. The same is true of the International Monetary Fund: some of the most skeptical analyses of the Fund's policies come from its own researchers, whose work has little if any discernible impact on IMF policy. See in particular the studies collected in Mario Blejer and Ke-young Chu, eds., *Fiscal Policy, Stabilization, and Growth in Developing Countries* (Washington, D.C.: International Monetary Fund, 1989).

3. Joseph A. Stiglitz, "Whither Socialism? Perspectives from the Economics of Information" (Wicksell Lectures, Stockholm, Sweden, 1990), and "The Invisible Hand and Modern Welfare Economics" (National Bureau of Economic Research, Working Paper no. 3641, 1991).

4. Robert E. Lucas, Jr., "On the Mechanics of Economic Development," *Journal of Monetary Economics* 22 (1988): 3-42.

5. Stiglitz, "Whither Socialism?" 12.

6. Kenneth Arrow and Georges Debreu, "Existence of an Equilibrium for a Competitive Economy," *Econometrica* 22 (1954): 256-90.

7. Arrow, "The Role of Securities in the Optimal Allocation of Risk-Bearing," *Review of Economic Studies* 31 (1964): 91-96.

8. Bruce Greenwald and Joseph E. Stiglitz, "Externalities in Economies with Imperfect Information and Incomplete Markets," *Quarterly Journal of Economics* 90 (1986): 229-64.

9. This discussion follows almost verbatim Luiz Carlos Bresser Pereira, José Maria Maravall, and Adam Przeworski, *Economic Reform in New Democracies* (New York: Cambridge University Press, 1992), where the reader can find evidence for the points developed here.

10. Stanley Fischer et al., eds., *Lessons of Economic Stabilization and Its Aftermath* (Cambridge: MIT Press, 1991), 404-5.

11. Vito Tanzi, "Fiscal Policy, Stabilization, and Growth," in Blejer and Chu, eds., op. cit., 30.

12. See the exchange between Bradford DeLong and William Baumol concerning "Productivity Growth, Convergence, and Welfare" in *American Economic Review* 78 (1988): 1138-59.

13. See Lucas, op. cit.; Gary Becker et al., "Human Capital, Fertility, and Economic Growth," *Journal of Political Economy* 98 (1990): 12-38; and Paul M. Romer, "Endogenous Technical Change," *Journal of Political Economy* 98 (1990): S71-S103.

14. Peter Murrell, "Can Neoclassical Economics Underpin the Reform of Centrally Planned Economies?" *Journal of Economic Perspectives* 5 (1991): 59-76.

15. Gene Grossman, "Promoting New Industrial Activities: A Survey of Recent Arguments and Evidence," *OECD Economic Studies* 14 (Spring 1990): 87-125.

16. Robert Barro, "Government Spending in a Simple Model of Endogenous Growth," *Journal of Political Economy* 98 (1990): S103-25; Ronald Finlay, "The New Political Economy: Its Explanatory Power for the LDCs," *Economics and Politics* 2 (1990): 193-221.

17. See George Stigler, *The Citizen and the State: Essays on Regulation* (Chicago: University of Chicago Press, 1975); and Robert D. Tollison, "Rent Seeking: A Survey," *Kyklos* 35 (1982): 575-602.

18. The seminal formulation of this problem is Leonid Hurwicz, "The Design of Resource-Allocation Mechanisms," *American Economic Review* 63 (1973): 1-30.

19. *Gazeta wyborcza* (Warsaw), 13 July 1990 (italics added).

20. Adam Przeworski, "Party Systems and Economic Development," Ph.D. dissertation, Northwestern University, 1966; Irma Adelman and Cynthia Morris, *Society, Politics, and Economic Development* (Baltimore: Johns Hopkins University Press, 1967); William G. Dick, "Authoritarian versus Nonauthoritarian Approaches to Economic Development," *Journal of Political Economy* 82 (1974): 817-27; Samuel P. Huntington and Jorge I. Dominguez, "Political Development," in F.I. Greenstein and N.W. Polsby, eds., *Handbook of Political Science*, vol. 3 (Reading, Mass.: Addison-Wesley, 1975); Robert M. Marsh, "Does Democracy Hinder Economic Development in the Latecomer Developing Nations?" *Comparative Social Research* 2 (1979): 215-48; Erich Weede, "The Impact of Democracy on Economic Growth: Some Evidence from Cross-National Analysis," *Kyklos* 36 (1983): 21-39; Roger C. Kormendi and Philip G. Meguire, "Macroeconomic Determinants of Growth," *Journal of Monetary Economics* 16 (1985): 141-63; Atul Kohli, "Democracy and Development," in John P. Lewis and Valeriana Kallab, eds., *Development Strategies Reconsidered* (New Brunswick: Transaction Books, 1986); Daniel Landau, "Government and Economic Growth in the Less-Developed Countries: An Empirical Study for 1960-1980," *Economic Development and Cultural Change* 35 (1986): 35-76; John Sloan and Kent L. Tedin, "The Consequences of Regime Type for Public-Policy Outputs," *Comparative Political Studies* 20 (1987): 98-124; Marsh, "Sociological Explanations of Economic Growth," *Studies in Comparative International Research* 13 (1988): 41-76; Abbas Pourgerami, "The Political Economy of Development: A Cross-National Causality Test of the Development-Democracy-Growth Hypothesis," *Public Choice* 58 (1988): 123-41; Gerald W. Scully, "The Institutional Framework and Economic Development," *Journal of Political Economy* 96 (1988): 652-62; Robert J. Barro, "A Cross-Country Study of Growth, Saving, and Government" (NBER Working Paper 2855, 1989); Kevin B. Grier

and Gordon Tullock, "An Empirical Analysis of Cross-National Economic Growth, 1951-80," *Journal of Monetary Economics* 24 (1989): 259-76; Karen Remmer, "Democracy and Economic Crisis: The Latin American Experience," *World Politics* 42 (1989-90): 315-35; Pourgerami, "The Political Economy of Development: An Empirical Investigation of the Wealth Theory of Democracy," *Journal of Theoretical Politics* 3 (1991): 189-211.

21. Brendan O'Flaherty, "Why Are There Democracies? A Principal-Agent Answer," *Economics and Politics* 2 (1990): 133-55.

22. Allan H. Meltzer and Scott F. Richard, "A Rational Theory of the Size of Government," *Journal of Political Economy* 89 (1981): 914-27.

23. Mackintosh and Ricardo are quoted in Stefan Collini et al., *That Noble Science of Politics* (Cambridge: Cambridge University Press, 1983), 98, 107.

24. Thomas Babington Macaulay, *Complete Writings* (20 vols., Boston and New York: Houghton-Mifflin, 1900), 17:263-76.

25. Karl Marx, *The Class Struggle in France, 1848 to 1850* (Moscow: Progress Publishers, 1952), 62.

26. Brian Barry, "The Continuing Relevance of Socialism," in idem, *Democracy, Power, and Justice: Essays in Political Theory* (Oxford: Oxford University Press, 1989), 529; Diane Elson, "Socialization of the Market," *New Left Review* 172 (1988), 3-44.

27. Among the seven countries compared in the most careful research on this topic to date, the percentage of persons who are poor after taxes and transfers is 4.8 (195,000) in Norway, 5.0 (410,000) in Sweden, 6.0 (3.23 million) in West Germany, 8.8 (1.61 million) in the United Kingdom, 12.1 (2.88 million) in Canada, 14.5 (446,000) in Israel, and 16.9 (36.88 million) in the United States. These figures are from Timothy Smeeding et al., *Poverty, Inequality, and Income Distribution in Comparative Perspective* (Washington, D.C.: The Urban Institute, 1990).

28. This is true of Eastern Europe as well. The Soviet Union did attempt to impose its own political institutions and economic integration on its satellites in Eastern Europe, yet the model of economic development there was to a large extent autarkic: even Stalinist development produced large steel mills in each country. Moreover, insofar as this model was internationalist it turned out to be unworkable, precisely because it came up against national aspirations.

6.
SOCIALISM, CAPITALISM, AND MODERNITY

G.M. Tamás

G.M. Tamás is director of the Institute of Philosophy of the Hungarian Academy of Sciences and a member of the Hungarian parliament. Born in Romania (Transylvania), he was exiled to Hungary in 1978, where he became lecturer and senior research fellow in the department of philosophy at the University of Budapest. Fired for political reasons, he became one of Hungary's leading dissidents and wrote extensively in samizdat. He has published numerous books and essays, and his work has been translated into 11 languages. He was elected to the parliament in 1990, and is chairman of the national committee of the Free Democratic Alliance (Liberal opposition).

Western socialists who do not wish to be seen as apologists for tyranny may dispute whether "actually existing socialism" was socialism at all. Yet the parallels between Western democratic and Eastern revolutionary-despotic socialism are numerous enough to allow us to assert that socialism is one of the main strategies of modernity, indeed, the only one which is (or was) global. It is the only variant of modernity that East and West have in common; otherwise, the twain shall never meet.

The communist parties of Europe were born out of impotent rage against the First World War. Reformist trade unions and social democratic parties had failed to keep the international proletariat from killing one another in the service of their respective capitalist-imperialist masters. Class solidarity melted in the heat of nationalist frenzy. Marxist leaders of the social democratic center had no moral theory of war. Revolutionary antimilitarism ("defeatism") turned against social democracy in three important respects: 1) The incipient communist movement led by Lenin and Rosa Luxemburg refused to regard social equality as the main goal of the workers' movement, maintaining instead that the suppression of alienation was the true essence of socialist politics. Thus did the Zimmerwald-Kienthal revolutionaries break with the idea of "working within the system" to achieve social justice and a better way of life for proletarians. They envisioned an immediate end to wage slavery and the division of labor as part of the revolution that would end all revolutions. 2) Because the proletarians themselves and their political representatives had proven unreliable, the "revolutionary subject" would henceforth be not the "empirical" working class itself, but rather the agent of its ideal essence as a class, the disciplined and self-conscious vanguard Party. 3) The liberal democratic illusion shared by the treacherous trade union leaders would be dispensed with, and Marx's vague notion of the "dictatorship of the proletariat" revitalized.

The messianic-revolutionary writers of the 1920s (Aleksandr Blok, Isaac Babel, Boris Pilnyak, Andrei Bely, and others) captured the prevailing sense of anticipation of the Last Battle that would overturn all previous orders and mark the rise of a new breed of healthy young barbarians to replace the corrupt old gentlemen who had sacrificed the flower of Europe's youth to the imperial system handed down by the Congress of Vienna. This sense that nothing was ever to be the same gripped figures as disparate as Spengler and Lenin, Mussolini and Béla Kun, Hitler and Trotsky. For their generation there was but one reality: war, a view most admirably described by Ernst Jünger, especially in his great essay *Der Arbeiter*. The skull beneath the skin of politics was armed force commanded by blind will.

War was hated, but somehow expressed the truth of things. The ennui and disillusionment of the sad uniformed assassin made him ridicule any concept of law, any hope of liberty, any attempt to distinguish between naked power and legitimate authority. The veterans who had seen the ideals of liberal individualism die on the battlefields had very simple ideas about a just society. Justice was personified by the brave lieutenant who shared his tinned meat, his flask of brandy, and his bottle of aspirin with his men, and was ready as well to share their death in a long and meaningless war of attrition. In their view, the civilian world that had sat back peacefully while they bled in the stinking trenches deserved only contempt. This idea was shared by such Westerners as Siegfried Sassoon, Robert Graves, Ernest Hemingway, Henri Barbusse, Hans Carossa, Erich Maria Remarque—and John Maynard Keynes. The Bolshevik generation did not consist of Bolsheviks alone. All its members shared a disgust for what they saw as the sham ideals of liberal humanism, altruistic patriotism, and the like. A new society would have to be forged by disenchanted veterans, united by a common sense of betrayal; filled with distrust for individuality, conventional politics, conventional morality, and *la patrie*; and overcome by loathing for bankers, dukes, politicians, generals, poets, philosophers, and columnists.

Thus did radical defeatism help to shape Bolshevism, a hostile new sibling to social democracy and "revisionist" (i.e., reformist-gradualist) Marxism that hated all Fabians for their fondness for "the system," that vile redoubt of servility, nationalism, military frenzy, cravings for rank and respectability, prosaic notions of civic duty, and "parliamentary cretinism."

But in spite of all these differences—the stressing of which gave the communists their impetus and explains quite well their suicidal insistence on continuing the fight against moderate socialists even at the moment of the Nazi takeover—the profound similarities remain. Above all, socialists of all colors—from pink to deep purple—were and still are progressives.

Marxism and Modernization

In Central and Eastern Europe socialists and communists alike faced a power structure based on an incomplete capitalism, where modern techniques for waging mechanized mass war (redistribution, government direction of industry and research, etc.) were grafted onto the body of a society that leftists regarded as "semifeudal" and that still featured great estates, quasi-aristocratic military castes, and old habits of social deference, religious piety, and humility toward the "superior state" (*Obrigkeitstaat*). It was not only liberal capitalism that exterminated those old ways, but the soldierly egalitarianism of the death-filled trenches.

Socialists of all shades also shared Marx's enthusiasm for demiurgic capitalism, the demonically creative force (known as such already by Milton, Blake, and Byron) that had opened up the closed medieval world and convinced progressives from Saint-Simon and Bentham to Engels and Spencer that it was both the best and worst of all possible social and economic arrangements. Capitalism's superiority, they thought, lay especially in its capacity to bring about a more rational organization of human resources, reduce personal servitude, break the grip of rigid status and prestige groups, and speed up scientific, technological, and economic development. It had changed a sleepy world of static provincialisms into a cosmos of unbridled dynamism. Socialists had always favored rapid economic growth, and the First World War persuaded them that a very potent central state would be the best vehicle for the rational reconstruction of society—one that would preserve the dynamism of capitalism while putting a final end to alienation. We should not forget that social democrats also advocate just such a state, though they are too cautious and humane to employ violent means of building it.

While Anglo-Saxon and Scandinavian socialists were preoccupied by inequality and class prejudice, their Continental comrades from Jean Jaurès and Jules Guesde to Lenin and Georg von Lukács wanted to end reification and alienation. The socialist revolutionaries of the East wanted to abolish not only inequality, but social roles as such.

Millenarian rebels have always refused to believe that God has ordained the differences among people; their attacks on the ancient Indo-

European division of society into castes of warriors, priests, and laborers (the Aryan social trinity as shown in the works of Georges Dumézil and Louis Dumont) were not—and this is the crucial point—directed against hierarchical differences alone, but against *any* plurality of human pursuits: specialization, separate social roles, and group loyalties all contradict the old myth of Universal Man. In Russia, both Narodniks and Bolsheviks condemned both social hierarchy and social pluralism as equally *artificial*: the only "natural" state was homogeneity, the metaphysical unity of the "species being" (*Gattungswesen*), Man who is identical with Humanity.

The divine legitimation for the plurality of social roles that had been provided by the Indian, Greco-Roman, and Germanic pantheons—and with them the old Aryan social trinity—had been subverted by monotheism. Similarly, liberal pluralism was subverted by socialism. The latter's denial of the natural givenness of plural spontaneity struck squarely at the heart of the Whig creed, which held (following Bernard Mandeville and Adam Smith) that the end result of individual action, whatever its motive, is for the best, and that the acceptance of difference is conducive both to liberty and to a morally dignified state of affairs. But this view, being only moral and not theological, never had quite the authority of the older, religiously based belief in the rightness of social differentiation. (Only Hegel attempted to overcome this difficulty.)

Modern revolutionary socialism is original in making the assumption—which it does not share with Narodniks and other romantics—that capitalist dynamics will help to bring about the end of *both* hierarchy and the division of labor. In a way, Lenin and his comrades were right. Liberal capitalism, after all, has encouraged social mobility, breaking up closed status groups, fostering democratic political participation, and softening the once-rigid boundaries of various elites. Economic growth made possible a grand rapprochement between classes: the unbridgeable gulf between serf and lord has been replaced by the much smaller distance between office clerk and factory worker; the self-made man appeared as a definite social type. Romantics wanted to realize the Unity of Man by *destroying* modernity; revolutionary socialists wished to attain the same goal by *using* modernity. Scientific technology, economic expansion, and mass culture were to become the uniquely modern means for realizing the age-old dream of Universal Man, a plebeian version of the Renaissance dream.

In many East European countries, this socialist view was the most positive picture of liberal capitalism that people ever encountered. In Russia, Czarist traditionalists, Slavophiles, and revolutionary Narodniks were as one in condemning frivolous Western modernity; only Marxists called for technology, science, rationalism, and industrialization. East European adversaries of Western-style liberal capitalism had few actual liberals or capitalists to oppose, but could find one real enemy: the

Bolsheviks. The paucity of Whiggish types in Russia also helped to determine Lenin's strategy of using the socialist state instead of the capitalist bourgeoisie as the instrument of modernizing change. The new state would initiate industrial development and make social roles interchangeable among groups and during one's lifetime. Anything that might stand in the way of this utopia—the family, religion, class, high culture—would be destroyed. Everything was to withdraw into the anonymity of the collective.

What historians often overlook is that Bolshevism did forge a modern society of sorts, while modernity was refused by the Bolsheviks' main rivals. With the death of East and Central European liberalism in 1917-18, no other modernizing agency was left. Class-conscious social democrats fought capitalism because, unlike their hostile communist twins, they actually did represent the starving workers. Conservatives retreated into romantic-feudal daydreaming and anti-Semitic mindlessness. The Church entertained a romantic vision of Christian socialism that revived prejudices against banking and interest quite à la Khomeini. The disaffected officer corps wanted simple justice. The peasant parties demanded cooperatives and, like farmers' groups always and everywhere, guaranteed income. Social democrats struggled to make capitalism accept reforms designed to promote "social justice" understood as greater equality, but capitalism had scarcely come to Eastern Europe. Communists wanted to create an industrial machine in order to conquer Paradise.

East European revolutionary socialism was as confused by the dilemmas of modernity as Western liberalism was at the time, but Bolshevik thaumaturgy has to a certain extent succeeded. John Lukacs's disturbing new book *The Duel* says that we are all national socialists even though Churchill and the Allies defeated the original bearers of that name in 1945.[1] Some combination of ethnic nationalism and collectivist welfarism characterizes most of the states in the world today; the disastrous consequences predicted by Friedrich Hayek are fended off only by the dogged resistance of cultural forces left over from the past—but only in the West, if there. The dirty work of modernization, which was done in England by *laissez-faire* liberalism and in Germany by the Prussian state and military industry, was performed in Eastern Europe and large parts of Asia by various versions of state socialism. What Stalin wrought—with labor camps, forced collectivization, mass deportations, wholesale murder, and the ruthless exploitation and destruction of natural resources—is a gigantic, if terrible, achievement.

Modernity East and West

The differences within the character of modernity in many regions of the world depend chiefly on *when* modernity hit them. The end of closed status groups, secularization, pluralism, the need for power to be of transparent legitimacy, mass education, and so on came to Eastern Europe with the advent of socialism, as did industrial technology, notions of deferred gratification and "life-plan" rationality, and scientific discourse. The problem facing Eastern Europe at this moment is not whether and how to introduce capitalism (or as we coyly call it, the "market economy"), but whether the dominant political forces here do or do not want to preserve the achievements of modernity that were brought to the West by liberalism and the Industrial Revolution—and that came to us on the bayonets of the Red Army.

Let us dwell for a moment longer on the nature of the communist utopia. I have—at the risk of being prosaic—translated the idea of an end to alienation as an end to fixed social roles. Here the communist utopia appears to be double-edged. What appeared futuristic to Western revolutionary socialists (whose overwhelming experience was of "capitalist anarchy," "atomization," and "aimlessness") appeared quite traditional to their Eastern counterparts, who saw this utopia as a potential *antidote to the West*. But this antidote, in contradistinction to merely feudal-romantic views, also offered a way to defeat the West with some of its own weapons. East European antiliberals and antimodernists of both the left and the right first saw Marxian revolutionary socialism as offering the advantage of being strong—something that the East needed because of its weakness vis-à-vis the colonizing, expansive West. But then an even greater advantage became apparent. Contacts with the Western Enlightenment under such reformers as Czar Peter the Great and Emperor Joseph II had undermined the old tribal-sacral legitimacy of the state in Central and Eastern Europe; national Jacobin and liberal nationalist turbulence (as in the Decembrist revolt of 1825 and the revolutions of 1848) sapped it further. Official legitimizing ideologies thenceforth became unhappy mixtures of sacralistic phrases and utilitarian arguments. But utilitarian arguments proved subversive of monarchic rule. Revolutionary socialism, however, could help to show that the suppression of social diversity was both useful as a tool of development *and* in tune with the natural (i.e., ancient) order of things.

The utilitarian character of revolutionary socialist argumentation helps to explain the sectarian struggles within communist parties. The "deviationists," "revisionists," and "liquidators" of communist history—most famously, the Trotskyites and Maoists—could always ask whether the twin revolutionary goals of "community" and "development" were best served by whatever tactics the Politburo and the Central Committee thought fit. The utilitarian side of socialist theories of legitimacy and authority was to become a trap for Bolshevik parties: there was no intrinsic reason why they should squash criticism, for they always said that their brand of rule was demonstrably better than others.[2] Both utilitarian antiutopianism and the critique of utilitarian-pragmatic tactics in the name of utopia could be silenced only by force: socialists have always been restive under socialist rule.

Modernity hit Western Europe when the dominion of Christianity was not in serious doubt; indeed, modernity was most successful when the pagan whimsies of the French Revolution had been defeated by the bastions of the *ancien régime*, Britain and Austria. The grand narrative of Western modernity is the remarkable story of how aristocratic tradition (based on Judeo-Christian theology, Greco-Roman ethics and statecraft, and the Aryan social trinity) gradually absorbed plebeian liberal capitalism, science, technology, urbanism, and the dissolution of spiritual and political bondage. This process of absorption of the emerging bourgeoisie has done more for modern society than all the Encyclopaedists, Jacobins, *carbonari*, and Freemasons taken together. For as it proceeded in its piecemeal, unideological, chaotically pragmatic way, it never directly raised the problem of *legitimacy*, but replaced it with that of *authority*. One of the unintended results was that people west of the Rhine could not address directly the quandary of the *state* as such; they thought instead in terms of law and government. State is a characteristically German and Russian idea, not a British or an Austrian one.

British and Austrian conservatism revered religion less as dogma than as ancient custom (this is what I called elsewhere the difference between *tradition* and *canon*, that is, tradition as truth and tradition as tradition). Religion thus understood was the opponent of utopia. Gradually everything within the Christian framework had become respectable religion; urgent theological disputes were sacrificed to an effective censorship operating in the name of a Hobbesian toleration, and one of the *old* wellheads of utopianism was thus capped. The merger of chivalric-baronial aristocracy and *noblesse de robe*, of haute bourgeoisie and high bureaucracy; the domestication of Christian religiosity into pietistic convention; even the democratic gains achieved by the extension of the franchise and social-welfare legislation—all helped to make possible the deferral of doubts about legitimacy, and the burden of proof shifted. The great liberal-conservative compromise of the nineteenth-century West limited political argument to the well-educated elite, where many convictions were left unspoken and the fragile balance was maintained by English flippancy and insincerity. The odd assortment of people who did dare to think about the fundamentals of civilization—Lord Salisbury, the Tractarians, Samuel Butler, George Eliot, and that redoubtable leveller David Lloyd George—were more or less marginalized; even the agonizings of Matthew Arnold went largely unheeded. Yet this Austro-British hypocrisy could not and did not hold. Faced with the universalistic moral challenge hurled at it by socialism, it had to seek the approval of the abstract political community; the result was the rise of universal suffrage and mass democracy. These destroyed the fragile pretense of pseudoaristocratic and pseudo-Christian liberal capitalism, while the First World War and its turbulent aftermath shattered the Burkean dream of gently gradual change. Still, this perhaps serendipitous constellation of circumstances worked for a long time to condition the idea that Westerners themselves had of modernity. A process of wild expansion, raucous dynamism, and harsh social dislocations went on under the genteel tutelage of institutions and habits of old.

But the process of unifying the upper-middle class and enlarging the aristocracy succeeded only in Britain; the Austro-Hungarian empire started down this road too late and too slowly to save itself. The Habsburgs presided over two middle classes: the so-called gentry composed of squires, senior civil servants, and army officers; and the despised bourgeoisie of private businessmen, bohemians, new professionals, shopkeepers, and those most important people of independent means (*Privatieren*). Those who belonged to this latter half of the middle class saw themselves as represented by social democracy and radicalism (if they belonged to some oppressed ethnic group), or else by anti-Semitic and chauvinistic Christian Socialism. In either case, they rejected the noble Whiggish liberalism of the cosmopolitan-aristocratic upper crust. Throughout the East, bourgeois groups were seen as aliens: Jews and Germans in Russia or the eastern half of Austria-Hungary; Muslims and Parsees in India; Chinese in Southeast Asia; East Indians in Africa and the British West Indies; Christians in Turkey or the Arab Middle East. The problem of capitalism in the East was—and has largely remained—*an ethnic and denominational problem*, just as it was in the pre-Enlightenment West. Socialism promised to suppress these disreputable social islets of capitalism, and thus easily lent itself to reactionary ethnic uses, whether indirectly (as in the case of Lenin) or openly (as in that of Hitler). Socialism promised a modernity that would replace both the stagnant *ancien régime* and the hated bourgeois-alien islets within it. Socialism promised to make capitalist-style dynamism compatible with the old-fashioned, indeed, archaic urge to suppress plurality. It kept this promise, too, but at a fearfully high cost. Far from being a surface phenomenon, socialism wrought a deep and lasting transformation of cultural and social life throughout Eastern Europe.

"Community" versus "Development"

The romantic-populist forces that dominate contemporary Eastern Europe are correct in seeing capitalism and socialism (both of which they oppose) as a single problem. When Western leftists bemoan the "universal triumph" of capitalism and "unmask" the Brave New World of McDonald's, they do not realize that they are acting as unwitting allies of the East European far right. The latter hates capitalism no less than they do, and its opposition to collectivist ideas is at best lukewarm.

All the attempts that were made to bring modernity to presocialist Eastern Europe failed dismally. Only revolutionary socialism made headway in this gargantuan task: industrialism and economic growth; electrification and mass transport; the division of space and time into units of equal size (East European peasants did not have watches and clocks until the 1950s); the documentation of administrative decisions; the regularization of legal procedure (even advanced Hungary did not have a penal code until the 1960s); the cessation of personal servitude (in the 1970s, a peasant in the mountains of Romania kissed my hand because I was wearing "town trousers"); mandatory education and mass literacy; the dissemination of scientific and humanistic learning; printed and electronic mass media; organized sports; modern health care and public hygiene; the separation of the workplace from the living quarters; the spread of the nuclear family; artificial contraception and legalized abortion—this whole catalogue of modern changes is one that East Europeans rightly associate with socialism.

All this was achieved through unimaginable violence wielded with unprecedented ruthlessness by those fanatical soldiers of change, the Red commissars. The zillions of "Marxist" seminars, indoctrination classes, and semimilitary professional-training courses not only served the purpose of ideological brainwashing, but also drilled masses of backward peasants in the ways of modernity, from reading a clockface and washing one's feet daily to the doctrines of Newton, Darwin, and Marx (taught by people who might have preserved a belief or two in witches and werewolves). Labor camps, long stretches of cruel military service, interminable after-work Party meetings, mandatory self-criticism and study sessions, Young Pioneers' summer camps, voluntary work detachments, Stakhanovite movements, and all the rest had a pervasive effect. Permanent mobilization for socialism aimed openly at the destruction of private life combined with super-Victorian prudery and cultural "conservatism" (middlebrow conventionalism); the accompanying symptoms were exhaustion, puritanical poverty, and a barbaric new lay mythology. New managerial elites were chosen on the basis of party loyalty, moral probity, and total political subservience. Every perk, promotion, and preferment was given by the party-state according to a political notion of "merit."

When reformers tried to introduce a modicum of economic rationality into the Stalinist model of development, they were resisted by many forces—and the history of this resistance explains many a feature of the contemporary confusion in Eastern Europe. This story is very well summarized by the once famous but now forgotten debate of the early 1960s on whether or not there was alienation under socialism.

The claim that there *was* alienation in "actually existing" socialism meant two things at the same time. First, it meant that not everything was perfect under socialism—a boldly subversive, almost seditious, thesis. Second, it meant that economic reforms, by reestablishing the commodity-money and labor-wage relationships, had reintroduced the characteristically capitalist phenomenon of reification.

This incipient criticism of "real" socialism combined both utilitarian discontent with socialism's poor economic performance and paleo-Bolshevik discontent with the new differentiation of social roles spurred by economic reforms. Revolutionary socialism began by aspiring to both "community" and "development," but wound up adopting reforms that bolstered the latter at the expense of the former. The communist leadership wanted reforms, but could not renounce the rhetoric of "community" that it needed to justify totalitarian control. The Party eventually silenced this debate, but the schism between the advocates of "development" and the advocates of "community" remained. Here you have in a nutshell the origins of the contemporary political party structure of postcommunist Eastern Europe. The dominant romantic-populist-collectivist forces are the heirs of the "community" side in the alienation debate, while the pragmatic "liberals" of today trace their ancestry to the "development" camp. Both are in search of a more respectable ideological past, but this cannot fool the historian of ideas.

Anticommunism and Anticapitalism

The puzzle that the countries of Eastern Europe have yet to solve is whether they want to continue on the trajectory of modern development that socialist revolution and conquest started (and in another but less important sense arrested), or whether they want to try to restore some sort of fictional community erected on the doctrines of Rousseau and de Maistre.

Here I must introduce a cautionary note owing to the phenomenon of East European duplicity. Contemporary East European governments are desperately trying to please what they imagine to be the Western boss. In Hungary, for instance, the government is trying to appear social democratic in Austria, Christian Democratic in Germany, quasi-Gaullist in France, conservative in Britain, Reaganite in the United States, and liberal in the Netherlands; it is none of these, of course, but it is more or less believed everywhere by gullible and ignorant Western observers and politicians, which is just as well. This caution is important because duplicity can sometimes confuse East Europeans themselves. The authority of Western ideas played an important part in the 1989 changes, but at the same time the old servile habit of imitation, of immediately accepting a language not of one's own making, also plays a curious role. It creates more resentment in a region already beset by anti-Western sentiment, especially on the right.

Deciphering contemporary East European political discourse means playing a very complicated hermeneutical game. Everybody speaks of "privatization," for instance, but most of them are really talking about renationalization through various cross-shareholding and cross-ownership schemes wherein the state remains the ultimate proprietor even as the fashionable etiquette of "the market" is being observed. Everybody also talks about getting rid of the old communist *apparatchiki*, but in practice this can mean anything from reshuffling various groups of holdover functionaries to imposing media censorship or carrying on the old fight between "development" and "community" factions by other means. All this obscures the truth of events in Eastern Europe from foreign observers and policy makers, who often wind up backing this or that political figure or group on a whim without really understanding what is going on (and what is going on is indeed quite difficult to grasp).

The main debate in Eastern Europe, meanwhile, is one familiar to those who know the history of intracommunist squabbles in the 1930s: it is the argument over heritage.

Since "communism" as such is thoroughly compromised and there is an official consensus (not shared by public opinion) that it was all bad, the debate is carried on in code. At its heart is the question of whether the old modernizing-reformist managerial elite should be replaced at the price of retarding economic change and strengthening state interference in the economy; or whether the economic reforms that began before the democratic turn of 1989 should be vigorously pursued at the price of keeping parts of the old "communist" (technocratic-professional) elite in place. Advocates of the second option argue that a British-style process of "absorption" will gradually (in a Burkean way) bring into being a new ruling class molded out of new and old elements while simultaneously helping East European society to make smooth progress toward pluralism, individualism, and greater freedom. This gradualist model is sometimes called "communist" in Eastern Europe, while the "community" faction's efforts to arrest development, erect an authoritarian state, and create from above a new moneyed class permeated by ethnic nationalism are sometimes called "conservative." The debate's sharpest cutting edge is the question of purges. Neo-Whigs like myself oppose purges and screenings and political trials in part because we know that such efforts inevitably bring a disproportionate amount of power to those who conduct them (like the Jacobins and the Bolsheviks). The resulting atmosphere of suspicion, denunciation, and lust for spoils that is already present in some countries in the region is inimical to both the principles of liberal democracy and the smooth functioning of a modern economy.

Witch-hunts are obviously only a method. Eastern Europe's plebeian new right, with its penchant for screenings, purges, secret files, unproven denunciations, and resentment toward elites of any kind, is afraid of capitalism and liberal democracy. The restoration of rural, static, deferential, and backward Eastern Europe is its program. Its roots in the "community" side of the alienation debate can partly be deduced from the presence in its ranks of one-time "national communists" like those in Hungary who spent the 1960s attacking what they contemptuously dubbed "Frigidaire socialism." Their critique of modernity as atomized, reified, selfish, greedy, and so on, has not changed a whit. Yet the arguments of those on the other side have not changed a great deal either. They regard capitalism and liberal democracy only as a technical means to certain utilitarian ends, as the best method for improving living standards and fostering social peace. Genuine believers in the superiority of a free society are few and far between. Those who were on the "development" side of the alienation debate now call themselves "liberal," and there is something in this, since this side is kinder and gentler, more willing to accept impartial laws and procedures as the means for settling social conflicts, and less inclined to authoritarianism. Nonetheless, they do not generally represent what Westerners have come to expect when they hear the word "liberal," whether used in its nineteenth-century Whiggish or contemporary American sense.

Our traditions are strongly anti-individualistic; fear of spontaneity is present all along our political spectrum. The dissolution of the late-communist state gave birth to a unique—and it now appears, all too brief—moment of liberty, innovation, and diversity. Now we once again have indoctrination, mindless militancy, anti-Western and anticapitalist xenophobia, and revolutionary disregard for law—all brought to us by movements that shouted themselves hoarse calling for human rights just a few years ago. These movements have by now established a pattern of change whose twin engines are the personnel department with its confidential files and the screening commission with its chaotic hearings and dubious accusations. Censorship, cultural philistinism, intolerance, paranoia, and authoritarian demagoguery are all rampant.

In Eastern Europe today, says one acute Hungarian political scientist, "anticommunism" means anticapitalism. Since the managerial elite has initiated—and of course profited from—market reforms, and since this is the social stratum that is nowadays called "communist," the rhetoric of anticommunism is directed against the modernizing, incipiently bourgeois elements. All those who want a Burkean merger of elites are called "procommunist." State-orchestrated schemes in which state companies and state banks own one another, with civil servants and politicians dominating their boards, go forward under the rubric of "privatization." Genuine attempts at privatization, on the other hand, are condemned as "communist theft."

The Socialist Legacy

The legacy of socialism is of course mixed, and contrary to what countless Western columnists say, nationalism is part of it. Far from having been suppressed or destroyed by socialism, nationalism was always one of its leading features.

Bolshevik "national communism" is well known to historians, but is not taken sufficiently into account in most explanations of what is happening today. Tito and Ceauşescu embraced national communism because it served their unwillingness to share their power with the Soviet Union; Gomulka's version defended a sort of reform (but ended in the anti-Semitic debacle of 1968). Despite what Marx himself tended to believe, national Bolshevism is a necessary consequence of the revolutionary theory of alienation. The systematic suppression of divergent social roles necessarily created a unitary community under a strong state. Most communists before World War II still believed in the suppression of the state as well—the state bureaucracy was, after all, a *separate* stratum—but this heroic consistency did not survive their coming to power. With world revolution a far-off prospect at best, the unalienated community would have to be national. The idea of pure community and its concomitant anti-Western, antimodern, romantic nationalism was adopted at first unwillingly, but later quite deliberately by the ruling communist parties of Eastern Europe, and was used by them to charm the colonial-minded intelligentsia of the East European "periphery." Thus was spawned the very powerful strain of Rousseauan utopianism so prevalent among the "community" camp. We should keep in mind that this utopian strain is at its base hostile to institutions such as the law-governed state. Those in Eastern Europe today who call for a "community of nations rather than a community of states" (where nations mean ethnocultural groups, not political communities of citizens) are echoing those half-forgotten accents out of our murky past that made communism acceptable to both anarcholibertarians and authoritarians by appealing to their shared animus against impersonal institutions in general and the impersonal rule of law in particular.

In other words, "contemporary" nationalism in our region is really nothing new, nor are its proponents. Far from being something that was resurrected by recent democratic changes, it is a telltale sign of continuity. Civic patriotism is absent, advocated only by lonely humanists in ineffective essays.

Francis Fukuyama's famous hypothesis concerning the "end of history" rests on the assumption that liberal democracy is about to win the game.[3] Nothing could be further from the truth. The East European revolution launched in 1989 is one more rebellion against modernity (therefore against the West, which after all is the inventor of that ruthless modernizing strategy called socialism), and in this respect is similar to Khomeini's revolution in Iran or the Islamic *intégriste* movement in Algeria.

In his sadly forgotten book *The War Against the West*, Aurel Kolnai showed how German romanticism served as a basis for National

Socialism.[4] It is important to understand that the resistance to liberal democracy in Eastern Europe rests on no ethical arguments save one (if this can be considered ethical, as I think it can): namely, that liberal democracy is *alien*. Oswald Spengler said in 1918 that the trouble with German Liberals was not that they were liberal, but that they were *English*. This argument, I am sorry to say, prevails. Not long ago in Bucharest, Romania, there was a public demonstration against "Abroad" as such. The main complaint against socialism today—even in Russia!—is that it resulted from foreign conquest, or in other words, was a species of rule by agents of "Abroad." (In fact, communism created the first wholly indigenous elites in East European history, replacing the cosmopolitan imperial aristocracies of old.) The innocent Orient raped by the brutal and cunning Occident—this is the image that dominates discussion of both socialism and capitalism in Eastern Europe. Fukuyama's gray and unified world does not exist; the ancient tensions remain. The gullible West is disarming now, after the end of the Cold War's imperial balance of power, at the very moment when war in Europe is a bigger threat than at any time since 1945 (indeed, three actual wars are going on at the date of this writing).

The Plight of East European Liberalism

Eastern Europe's liberals are routinely accused of being in cahoots with the socialist left. They very seldom are, but the romantic-populist right sees clearly that they are both "Western" and modernist, which is enough to damn them both. The liberal movements are fighting a rearguard battle. This is not to deny that a democratic revolution did take place in Eastern Europe, but the democracy that came out of it is of the Jacobin variety: a majoritarian, plebiscitarian, antipluralistic democracy transfixed by the old socialist myth of direct participation. There is nothing about it that is liberal.

All the surveys and polling data show that public opinion in our region rejects dictatorship, but would like to see a strong man at the helm; favors popular government, but hates parliament, parties, and the press; likes social welfare legislation and equality, but not trade unions; wants to topple the present government, but disapproves of the idea of a regular opposition; supports the notion of the market (which is a code word for Western-style living standards), but wishes to punish and expropriate the rich and condemns banking for preying on simple working people; favors a guaranteed minimum income, but sees unemployment as an immoral state and wants to punish or possibly deport the unemployed. In one Hungarian poll, more than 80 percent of the respondents condemned communism as "evil," but when asked to name their favorite politicians, listed four former communist leaders among the top five. These results could be dismissed as a reflection of passing confusion, one of the temporary "difficulties of transition." To my mind, however, that would be a grave mistake. The opinions summarized above are characteristic of a situation that has not essentially changed since the emergence of revolutionary socialism.[5]

East Europeans still do not want to accept the "alienated" individualism and social diversity of liberal capitalism, but are unwilling to return to the kind of harsh, even tyrannical, rule that would be needed to forge essential unity. Are they really unique in this?

Some might say that all this represents a resurgence of "conservatism," but the rejection of modernity is not conservative. After all, it was not Burke but Robespierre who was unable to make his peace with modernity.

NOTES

1. John Lukacs, *The Duel* (London: Jonathan Cape, 1991).

2. As Leo Strauss noted in another context: "[T]he loathing of Utopias is conscious of its basis in more stringent intellectual discipline, in a deeper intellectual probity. The opposition to Utopia is thus nothing other than the opposition to religion. For religion too was rejected because it was held to have its foundation in wishing. Not wishing, but recognizing what is; not waiting for good fortune, but commanding fortune; therefore not making claims on fate, but loving fate; hence not making claims on men, on other men." *Spinoza's Critique of Religion* (New York: Schocken Books, 1965), 226.

3. Fukuyama's celebrated article in the Summer 1989 issue of *The National Interest* and his subsequent book, *The End of History and the Last Man* (New York: Free Press, 1992), are obviously indirect comments and variations on themes associated with Leo Strauss and his students. Indeed, it may be said that both the book and the essay that spawned it are an expanded version of a footnote in Allan Bloom, *The Closing of the American Mind* (New York: Simon and Schuster, 1987), 222n. That footnote, in turn, is unthinkable without the exchanges between Leo Strauss and Alexandre Kojève that are reproduced in Strauss's *On Tyranny*, rev. ed. (New York: Free Press, 1991). The connection was noticed by Pierre Bouretz, "Histoire et utopie (Fukuyama/Hegel, Mosès/Rosenzweig)," *Esprit*, May 1992, 119-33. Cf. Dominique Auffret, *Alexandre Kojève* (Paris: Grasset, 1990).

4. Aurel Kolnai, *The War Against the West* (New York: Viking Press, 1938).

5. The only serious theoretical work on the transition in Eastern Europe is Michel Henry's *Du communisme au capitalisme: théorie d'une catastrophe* (Paris: Odile Jacob, 1990). Although I do not agree with Henry's prejudices and political conclusions, his analysis is excellent. On his philosophical views, see Rolf Kühn, "Freiheits-'Dialektik' und immanente 'Nicht-Freiheit': Analyse des Situationsbegriffs nach Michel Henry," *Zeitschrift für philosophische Forschung* 46 (January-March 1992): 7-23. Another interesting radical view can be found in Zbigniew Rau, "The State of Enslavement: The East European Substitute for the State of Nature," *Political Studies* 39 (June 1991): 253-69. The radical economic program of "de-étatization" is best summarized in János Kornai, *The Road to a Free Economy: Shifting from a Socialist Society* (London and New York: W.W. Norton, 1991), which is still the best guide to the topic, even in this poor translation from the original Hungarian.

7.
IN DEFENSE
OF NEOLIBERALISM

Jeremy Shearmur

Jeremy Shearmur *has just joined the department of political science, faculty of arts, as a lecturer at the Australian National University in Canberra. Until May 1992, he was senior research fellow and director of studies at the Institute for Humane Studies and research associate professor at George Mason University. He received his Ph.D. from the London School of Economics, where he spent eight years as research assistant to Sir Karl Popper and wrote a dissertation on the political thought of Friedrich Hayek. He has also taught at the University of Edinburgh and the University of Manchester, and has served as director of studies at the Centre for Policy Studies in London.*

I will address my comments primarily to Adam Przeworski's wide-ranging essay on the relation between differing economic approaches and democracy. He offers much to give pause to those who are overly optimistic about the possibilities of a swift and easy transition to a decent, humane, and reasonably affluent social order in Central and Eastern Europe, or who think that it is obvious that developments there must lead to a benign combination of markets and democracy. Przeworski's reflections should also give pause to those who think that such a combination will necessarily work; most importantly, he reminds us of our ignorance.

Nonetheless, I do have some reservations. Although the essay is rather diffuse and pursues many different issues, its overall thrust is regrettably negative. It is understandable that Przeworski should be fed up with ideologically inspired overconfidence, but it is a shame that he stopped at pure critique when the problems at hand are so great and so pressing.

More seriously, I also have reservations about the adequacy of the criticisms he aims at "neoliberal ideology." Przeworski tells us that his observations "should not be construed as a defense of traditional patterns of state intervention, whether under capitalism or socialism; as an argument against relying on markets; or as an attack on promarket reforms." But in light of the contents of his essay, much of which is directed against what he takes to be the rationale for promarket approaches, this disclaimer seems to be largely *pro forma*. He advances a variety of considerations that appear to argue in favor of the state's playing a larger role in development. And he seems to suggest that it is, distinctively, neoliberals who are engaged in morally problematic experiments with the well-being of their fellow citizens.

Let us consider three topics that Przeworski discusses as he elaborates these criticisms: 1) market imperfections and Adam Smith's "invisible hand"; 2) the positive role of the state in bringing about economic development (a topic that moves Przeworski to ponder the advantages of the Swedish model); and 3) issues of pluralism and social "experiments" that affect the lives of actual human beings.

In his comments on market imperfections and Smith's invisible hand, Przeworski refers to well-known ways in which actual market institutions can fail to meet the conditions that are needed for the realization of general market equilibrium. He places particular emphasis on the imperfection of our knowledge—on human ignorance, in other words. This and other points that Przeworski makes are correct, but they in no way constitute a significant argument against the neoliberal view.

After all, it was Schumpeter's fellow Austrian, Friedrich Hayek, writing a little before the publication of *Capitalism, Socialism and Democracy*, who raised just this issue of human ignorance in the course of his argument about the insurmountable difficulties of economic calculation under socialism.[1] Hayek went on to explain how the limitations of human knowledge also posed difficulties for the notion of intertemporal general equilibrium, an idea with which he had previously been working. Hayek's own subsequent work, and that of many neoliberals who followed him, has referred precisely to human ignorance, to the disaggregated and sometimes tacit character of human knowledge, and to the importance of learning by trial and error in making the case for markets as opposed to the state.[2] Hayek, when discussing the problems that the imperfection of human knowledge posed for the idea of general equilibrium, also stressed that it was essentially an empirical matter as to which institutional arrangements would lead people's plans into coordination. This is not the place to discuss Hayek's work in any detail. Suffice it to say that the claim that the real world satisfies the assumptions of general equilibrium theory plays no role in the work of Hayek or, as far as I know, any other neoliberal defender of markets. (It is worth noting that there is virtually no mention in Przeworski's essay of the actual works of the neoliberals whom he criticizes.)

Przeworski presents the same points as telling against Adam Smith's famous idea of the "invisible hand." Yet it should be obvious to any careful reader of Smith that his case for markets is not based on a vision of modern welfare economics developed in the setting of general equilibrium. To give but one example, Smith's treatment of large-scale social transformations (e.g., his "four-stage" theory) makes it clear that such changes typically involve significant welfare losses for some people.[3] Rather, at the heart of Smith's vision is the idea that a commercial society may offer all its citizens both well-being and an unprecedented kind of liberty.[4] His claim was clearly that such a system, with all its admitted faults, was better than any of the available alternatives.

While it would of course be a mistake to treat Smith as if he were dealing with societies just like our own, much of what he says about commercial societies is still highly relevant to our situation. If one bolsters Smith with Hayek's emphasis on the significance of disaggregated decision making and the value of private property in dispersing power, one has something closer to the actual basis of the neoliberal argument. This argument clearly stands in need of further appraisal, both theoretical and empirical. But it remains largely untouched by the material concerning theoretical economics to which Przeworski refers, although his discussion of the empirical material on development promises to open up some rather interesting issues.

Social Experiments and the State

As for the positive role of the state and the attractions of Swedish-style social democracy, there is this to be said: If we are lucky, the state *might* play a positive role (there have been some impressive historical examples), but the state has also quite often been the source of immense harm. Moreover, there is the further question of whether we should give up our liberty to the state, even if we could gain materially by doing so. I might stand to gain from surrendering control over my diet and exercise to a kind of nanny, but I would prefer my freedom—even if I anticipate the possibility of abusing it—to a long, fit, and healthy life of tutelage.

If, nonetheless, we are tempted by Przeworski's argument to accord a positive role to the state, we need to confront some problems. First, we must respond to public choice theory's argument that we must not simply assume that the state will play the role of an all-knowing and benevolent despot. If the state is invoked to take care of "market failures," we need to be told how it is to identify what is needed, why we should expect that it will do what is needed, and why those with access to its power will not use this for other—and predatory—purposes. Unless this challenge is met, there seems to me no more rationale for offering us models within which the state and its functionaries are acting to correct market failures than there would be for models in which God and his angels are so doing. Przeworski refers to some of the public choice literature, but he offers no general response to it. This seems to me to limit severely the value of the cases he cites where the state has played a positive role in suggesting a general model upon which we can draw. Second, Przeworski's emphasis upon the importance of institutional design seems to me completely correct. But in my view, problems concerning the control of rent seeking would suggest that such activities should themselves be undertaken, as far as possible, within the private sector.

The kinds of problems that public choice theory has raised are germane to the current situation in Central and Eastern Europe. For there, after all, people have suffered under regimes that claimed, insistently, to be acting in the public interest—an experience which has surely led those people to be skeptical of the idea that state functionaries can genuinely be expected to serve the public interest. It is far from clear that we can expect the states of that region to play the kind of role that the state at its best has played in other, happier lands. In such circumstances, where there is ample reason to be distrustful of appeals to the public interest, the liberal tradition's search for forms of social cooperation that require only a minimal reliance on virtue seems particularly pertinent.

As for the Swedish model, it is not without its attractions. But when it worked, it seemed to depend on a lean, mean market economy whose surplus could be used for welfare (just as it was once used, in the Sweden of Gustavus Adolphus and Charles XII, for warfare). To advocate this model where productive market economies are nonexistent (as in Central and Eastern Europe) is like trying to build a house by starting with the roof and working downwards. The Swedish way also rests on some not easily reproducible social prerequisites, including ethnocultural homogeneity and forms of social control that people from non-Scandinavian cultures might find unacceptable. We cannot and should not treat any human beings—ourselves or others—as blank slates onto which instructions for any form of behavior can be written at will.

Przeworski, to his credit, is also concerned about the distance that separates leaders from led in Central and Eastern Europe, and he fears social experiments because they may hurt real people. There are problems here, certainly, but to cite them as points against current regimes or their advisors seems to me a little unfair.

The peoples of the postcommunist world are trying to rebuild their societies and their lives on the ruins of a vast and catastrophic social experiment. A leading trait of the regimes that carried out this experiment was hostility toward forms of social organization that were independent of the party and the state. It would thus be surprising if any succeeding regime did not face some difficulties caused by its distance from such autonomous organizations. Moreover, what has managed to survive from the old regime hardly seems to furnish the ideal ingredients for viable and humane societies.

Those like myself and Przeworski, who favor such viable and humane societies, must ask ourselves whether our ideals are to be forced onto others, and whether the kind of social experimentation against which Przeworski cautions us can be avoided. Indeed, given the degree to which neoliberal advocates of market-based social orders have stressed that such orders typically bring with them phenomena that citizens find unattractive, anyone who favors market-based social reforms (including those who wish for a measure of state action or even some sort of "market-based democratic socialism") must face the problem of how such reforms are to be legitimated in the eyes of East and Central European peoples.

In this context, G.M. Tamás's remarks about the kinship that socialism and liberalism share as alternative versions of modernity are particularly telling, even if somewhat embarrassing to a liberal antisocialist like myself. For the liberal—and indeed for anyone who cares about the plight of postcommunist countries—large-scale social change seems at once highly necessary and excruciatingly problematic. What precisely should be done is not clear, and those things that appear needful to the outside observer may not enjoy the support of people whose characters and expectations have been shaped by life under regimes of a radically different character.

Przeworski is right to direct attention to the vast extent of our collective ignorance. Yet he, no less than the neoliberals he criticizes, needs to acknowledge that this ignorance has implications for *any* proposed solution to the problems of postcommunist countries. Likewise, anyone with ideas (be they neoliberal or otherwise) about how best to shape the future of those countries must also face the challenge of gaining legitimation for his proposals.

The Proper Limits of Government

By way of concluding my comments, I would like to raise the rather heretical question of whether democracy is something of value in itself. Freedom, well-being, autonomy, companionship, cooperation—all these can lay plausible claim to intrinsic value. But *democracy?*

I am an implacable opponent of tyranny and authoritarianism. I also think that since governments make collective decisions on our behalf, we should be able to get rid of them by voting rather than fighting. Further, in many fields it is important that our ideals and opinions should be held up to open and public criticism. But it seems to me mistaken—and possibly damaging—to set democracy up as something that is valuable for its own sake. My worry is that people may thus be misled into thinking that anything can become legitimate simply by being the result of majority decision—a prospect that seems particularly worrisome in lands where there is no tradition of respect for individual liberty and where nationalism may lend a quasi-sacred cast to the will of the majority.

What matter, in my view, are individuals: their judgments, opinions, preferences, quirks, and habits, and above all their freedom—provided that all these are conceived and exercised in ways that respect the similar concerns of others. As Herbert Spencer put it: "The liberty which a citizen enjoys is to be measured, not by the nature of the governmental machinery he lives under, whether representative or other, but by the relative paucity of the restraints it imposes on him."[5]

> "...my personal preference would be for a transition to a regime that erects barriers against the state—the most frequent source of exploitation and coerced social experimentation in human history."

Even if the residents of Central and Eastern Europe became attached overnight to the goal of economic growth and agreed with Przeworski about how to attain it, large-scale change—and, in view of our ignorance, risky social experiments—would still be unavoidable. My own preference would be for a transition to regimes in which individual freedom, property rights, and the rule of law are secured on behalf of all. I would not wish these regimes to do any more (although I would favor other citizens assuming responsibility for assisting those who lived through the old regimes but are too old to start over).

In other words, my personal preference would be for a transition to a regime that erects barriers against the state—the most frequent source of exploitation and coerced social experimentation in human history. Such barriers need to be built around all governments, including democratic ones. (My earlier point about the merely instrumental value of democracy comes into play here. One of the more important tasks of intellectuals in democratic societies, I think, is to remind us of the proper limits of governments, democratic ones included.) Among other things, this would encourage the provision of many goods and services on a pluralistic basis—pluralistic because it is fully voluntary. This, I believe, might contribute to a rebirth of "intermediate institutions," the absence of which helps to cause the gap between rulers and ruled that so concerns Przeworski. Such ideas are admittedly somewhat speculative, although there are striking historical examples of the private provision of many sorts of things that most people today think can *only* be furnished by the state.[6] There is, certainly, a great deal to be said for systems in which ordinary people are as much as possible left free to trust their own judgment and act on the basis of their own practical knowledge.

Such a regime would be liberal, and thus anathema to most nationalists and religious antimodernists. But it would at least offer them something: the possibility of freely pursuing their own ways of life in a manner consistent with the liberty of others. This, I should add, might also contribute slightly to solving the problems of change and legitimation.

As a former student of Karl Popper, I welcome Przeworski's emphasis on our ignorance, and his warning against playing God with the lives of others. But I remain sorry that he fails to grasp that he is in the same boat with those whom he criticizes, and that he has little to say to those in Central and Eastern Europe who now have both the freedom and the immense responsibility of grappling with these historic challenges.

NOTES

1. See the essays collected in *Individualism and Economic Order* (Chicago: University of Chicago Press, 1946).

2. For example, see Hayek's "Competition as a Discovery Procedure," in his *New Studies in Philosophy, Politics, Economics, and the History of Ideas* (Chicago: University of Chicago Press, 1978), 179-90.

3. Consider, for example, Smith's discussion of the way in which, with the transition from hunting to herding as a mode of subsistence, there comes inequality and dependence of the poor upon the rich "because [the poor] could not now gain subsistence from hunting, as the rich had made the game, now become tame, their own property." "Report Dated 1766," in Adam Smith, *Lectures on Jurisprudence* (Oxford: Oxford University Press, 1978), 405.

4. For a striking overview of these issues, see Istvan Hont and Michael Ignatieff, "Needs and Justice in the *Wealth of Nations*," in idem, eds., *Wealth and Virtue* (Cambridge: Cambridge University Press, 1983), 1-44.

5. Herbert Spencer, *Man versus the State* (London: Williams and Norgate, 1885), 15-16.

6. For samples of the growing literature on this possibility, see Stephen Davies, "Edwin Chadwick and the Genesis of the English Welfare State," *Critical Review* 4 (Fall 1990): 523-36; Bruce Benson, *The Enterprise of Law* (San Francisco: Pacific Research Institute, 1991); and David Beito's two essays, "Mutual Aid for Social Welfare: The Case of American Fraternal Societies," *Critical Review* 4 (Fall 1990): 709-36; and "The Formation of Urban Infrastructure Through Non-Government Planning: The Private Places of St. Louis," *Journal of Urban History* 16 (May 1990): 263-303.

8.
WHY FREE MARKETS
ARE NOT ENOUGH

Robert A. Dahl

Robert A. Dahl *is Sterling Professor of Political Science (emeritus) at Yale University, where he has taught for more than 40 years. A past president of the American Political Science Association, he has received numerous awards for his writings, as well as honorary degrees from the University of Michigan and the University of Alaska. His many well-known books include* A Preface to Democratic Theory *(1956),* Who Governs? Democracy and Power in an American City *(1961),* Polyarchy: Participation and Opposition *(1971),* A Preface to Economic Democracy *(1985), and* Democracy and Its Critics *(1989).*

It is a striking and frequently noted fact that modern democracy has existed only in countries with economic systems in which production and distribution are mainly carried on by privately owned enterprises that are strongly oriented toward markets—that is, in countries with capitalist economic systems. Though not all capitalist countries are or have been democratic, all democratic countries have had capitalist economies.

This connection does not seem to me to be a historical accident. Elsewhere I have recently attempted to spell out the argument that modern democracy requires a market economy.[1] I believe that we have compelling reasons for concluding that a centrally directed command economy would provide political leaders with access to such powerful resources for persuasion, manipulation, and coercion as to make democracy extremely unlikely in the long term, no matter whether firms were collectively or privately owned. The only feasible alternative is some kind of market economy.

Might democracy be compatible, then, with a market economy based not on private but preponderantly on public, state, or social ownership? Schumpeter's solution, in which "the control over means of production and over production itself is vested with a central authority," seems to run risks very much like those of a command economy—as he himself was well aware.[2] The Yugoslav experience does not decisively settle the question of whether democracy might be compatible with a "socialist" market economy based on some form of decentralized "collective" or "social" ownership and control. After all, despite the extraordinary pluralism and decentralization of Yugoslavia, Tito and his successors were not liberal democrats; they insisted on maintaining the hegemony of the Party and the suppression of opposition political parties.

Let me assume, however, that democratic countries will have market economies in which economic enterprises are mainly privately owned. One theoretical possibility is that in democratic countries, markets will be, by and large, strictly competitive. Historically, however, no democratic country has steadily chosen this path. Here, I want to discuss several reasons why all democratic countries have rejected strictly competitive market economies in favor of mixed economies in which markets are significantly modified by state intervention.

In his excellent essay, Adam Przeworski shows why competitive markets are not necessarily efficient and may not necessarily lead to economic growth. As he also suggests, an additional defect of a strictly competitive market economy is its severe *moral* weaknesses. For even if competitive markets were to produce efficient outcomes, these efficient outcomes (in the sense of Pareto optimality) would not necessarily be justifiable; and some justifiable outcomes may be inefficient.

There are many reasons why an efficient outcome might reasonably be judged to be unjustifiable, but let us content ourselves with two very broad ones: justice (or fairness), and democracy. As to justice, one crucial example may suffice. We would be justified in accepting an efficient outcome as just or fair only on the heroic assumption, which is often stated and thereafter ignored, that the initial distribution of income and bargaining power was also just. An allocation of resources that is maximally efficient (Pareto optimal) is perfectly consistent with an indefinite number of different income distributions, ranging from perfect equality to the most extreme inequality. Thus the statement that unregulated competitive markets are a necessary means to "efficiency" and "socially optimal" outcomes, *and therefore desirable*, is morally trivial unless it is further grounded in an argument about the justice and feasibility of alternative distributions of income and other crucial resources.[3]

As Przeworski points out, no small part of the effort to regulate markets has been stimulated by the attempt to alter the distribution of income. This is not to say that the results of these efforts have produced a fairer distribution of income (though if fairness requires less unequal incomes, then some countries have brought about a more just distribution of income). Nor is it to say that the methods chosen have necessarily been the most efficient ones available; on the contrary, they may often be highly inefficient, ineffective, and even perverse.[4] It is only to say that if one believes that the existing distribution of income is unjustified, then it is reasonable to attempt to obtain a more justifiable distribution through government intervention. Notice, too, that such an approach would be reasonable no matter whether one acts from altruism, public virtue, or rational self-interest.

Competitive Markets versus Democracy

There are also good reasons to conclude that the outcome of a system of competitive markets may be excessively harmful to the process and institutions of democratic government. Indeed, it is essential that these processes and institutions be insulated from the market—for example, by making it illegal to sell one's vote whether as citizen or legislator, or to sell one's services as a government official.

A second source of conflict between democratic processes and competitive markets arises because persons who believe themselves injured by the market will accept economically efficient (Pareto-optimal) outcomes as desirable only if they act not from rational self-interest but rather from a commitment to the general good. In older language, they would need to be moved by a strong sense of public virtue. Moving toward Pareto optimality does not guarantee that no one will be injured in the process. It merely specifies that once Pareto optimality has been achieved, any change would make some person worse off. Likewise, no other relevant criterion of the general good prescribes that no one will ever be harmed for the greater good of society. Nonetheless, if persons injured by market outcomes are confronted with the argument that the greater good of society requires a competitive market even if they themselves are injured in the process, they are likely to reply: "So what?"

Ironically, the assumption that society will benefit if everyone acts from motives of rational self-interest (in their economic transactions at any rate) stands in sharp contradiction to the requirement that the victims of competitive markets must somehow be prevented from acting selfishly in order for the optimal state of affairs to be reached. But if, in order to maximize the general welfare, victims must not act in their own self-interest, then they must either be deluded about their own interests, or else be willing to sacrifice them for the good of some larger entity.[5] Yet in a market society, as indeed perhaps in any large and heterogeneous society, prevailing cultural norms and practices are unlikely to encourage strong dedication to public virtue.

A third source of conflict between democracy and strictly competitive markets can be traced to the obvious truth that in some cases the argument for nonintervention is necessarily too abstract and recondite to be persuasive to the general public, not least to the victims. Much of the argument about efficiency, at least in the sense of Pareto optimality, is for most people literally incomprehensible. Even for intellectual and policy elites convinced of the desirability of strictly competitive markets, the costs of persuading those who disagree may prove prohibitive. History, at any rate, seems to show that this has generally been the case. In a democratic country the political elites may not be sufficiently independent of public opinion to carry out a policy that they believe to be rationally justified against the preferences of a substantial minority, let alone of a majority.

A final source of conflict arises from the high costs of *imposing* competitive market outcomes on people in a democratic country. If people who believe themselves to be injured by free markets cannot be persuaded by rational argument to accept their lot, they might be compelled to do so. Even in a democratic country, people are compelled to obey laws with which they disagree. After all, policies requiring government intervention to *alter* market relations, processes, and outcomes are not self-enforcing; ordinarily they are upheld by the threat, and often the enforcement, of coercion in the form of severe penalties for violating the laws and administrative rulings intended to carry out the interventionist policies. What is sometimes forgotten, however, is that government policies intended to *inaugurate, protect,* or *maintain* strictly free markets will also, as we have just seen, ordinarily require coercion.

In a country pretty much governed according to the principle of majority rule, a majority of citizens might come to believe in the theoretical or practical arguments advanced on behalf of the benefits of unfettered markets. Enough citizens to form a steady majority might conclude that their own interests are best served by strictly free markets for all economic resources; or a majority of citizens might be genuinely committed to serving the general good and believe that strictly free markets are necessary to it. Whatever the basis of their belief, we can imagine that they might be willing to support policies, and to insist that the government adopt and enforce policies, intended to avoid or prevent interference with the operation of strictly free markets. We can also imagine that they might be willing to bear the costs—moral, personal, social, political, economic—of enforcing these policies against the resistance of people who believe themselves harmed.

We can imagine still another possibility. In the real world of modern democracy (or what I prefer to call polyarchy) political elites often enjoy a considerable degree of autonomy. We might imagine, then, that leaders of a persistent majority coalition are strongly convinced of the importance of maintaining a system of strictly free markets, and are able to bring about the adoption of the appropriate policies without losing the support of a majority of voters, many of whom might not be convinced adherents of the policies of their political leaders.

But in the real world, compulsion is costly. People who are harmed by policies enforced against their will therefore have incentives for finding, inventing, and adopting actions, both individual and collective, that will prevent or undermine effective enforcement. Indeed, in liberal democratic systems it is often impossible for governments to enforce laws effectively against the resistance of a minority, or simply too costly for the effort to be seen as worthwhile. The question of when and how ruthlessly to enforce a law and when and how to yield to its opponents turns into a problem requiring political judgment. It is no longer a matter of abstract principle but of pragmatic decision, a weighing of relative costs and gains in a very broad sense.

Sources of Government Intervention

We know that government intervention is costly, and it is sometimes contended that the costs of government intervention in market decisions outweigh the benefits. Arriving at a defensible judgment is obviously enormously difficult.[6] The relevant point, however, is that intervention to create or protect markets is also costly; resistance and defiance can generate intolerably high costs. One has only to recall the attempts of governments, sometimes accompanied by violence, to prevent workers from forming trade unions and engaging in strikes and other collective actions.

Even more important than the costs of coercion required in order to maintain strictly free markets are the familiar dynamics of politics in democratic countries. The rules of the democratic game provide adult citizens with at least one resource that in the aggregate possesses great value for elected leaders—the vote. The rules of the game also ensure that many people enjoy access to the political arena in other ways. Political competition provides elected leaders with incentives for responding to the views and votes of any organized or unorganized aggregate of people numbering more than a handful of potential voters. If one set of competing leaders cannot fashion a response attractive to such a group without expecting to lose more support than it gains, another set of leaders may find it more profitable to take up their cause.

Majority coalitions are rarely if ever truly homogeneous; they are really coalitions of minorities, collections of people with converging or complementary but not perfectly identical concerns. These coalitions are far from stable in the long run. Hence people whose claims are ignored by the existing government coalition often stand a chance of having their claims taken more seriously by a future government coalition. Moreover, although the extent to which groups outside the incumbent governing coalition can influence government policies varies greatly among democratic countries, governments often accommodate themselves even to groups of voters who currently tend to give their support to the opposition.

One way or another, then, over time the victims of free markets are likely to influence the government—or *some* government, whether local, state, provincial, or regional—to adopt interventionist policies intended to protect them.

Given the evident impossibility of creating and maintaining a strictly free market, some proponents of free markets might conclude that the fault lies not in the policies themselves but in democratic processes that allow the unenlightened to prevail over the enlightened. They might even conclude that for the enlightened to prevail over the unenlightened on economic policy (and perhaps other matters as well), democratic processes and institutions should be replaced by guardianship or elite rule—or to put it more bluntly, by an authoritarian dictatorship. This is not the place to discuss the moral and political folly of such a view.[7] Perhaps the only point worth emphasizing here is that if a free-market economy can only be maintained by a nondemocratic political system, then the vision of nineteenth-century liberalism lies in utter ruins.

The upshot of all this is that every democratic country has rejected the practice, if not always the ideology, of unregulated competitive markets. Although it is true that a market economy exists in all democratic countries, it is also true that in every democratic country the market economy is modified by government intervention. These mixed economies take many different forms, from the corporatist systems of the Scandinavian countries, Germany, Austria, and the Netherlands to the more fragmented systems of Britain and the United States.[8] Moreover, the extent and forms of intervention vary not only from country to country, but also over time.

Neither historical experience nor theoretical considerations, then, provide grounds for believing that the complex patterns of government intervention and markets will ever be perfectly stable or substantially similar in all countries with market economies and democratic political systems. There is no convincing evidence that points to the existence of a Platonic ideal equilibrium toward which these various patterns converge. On the contrary, there are strong reasons for concluding that 1) different countries will continue to display different patterns of market competition, regulation, and intervention, and 2) the pattern within any particular country will continue to change together with changes in the society, the economy, the political forces, and the ideas, beliefs, perceptions, and values of its people.[9]

It is true that all democratic countries have rejected a centralized command economy as an alternative to a market economy; but they have also rejected a strictly free-market economy as an alternative to a mixed economy in which market outcomes are substantially modified by government intervention.

NOTES

1. Robert A. Dahl, "Why All Democratic Governments Have Mixed Economies," in John Chapman and Ian Shapiro, eds., *NOMOS* XXXV, *Community and Democracy* (New

York: New York University Press, 1992), from which the following comments are adapted. It is important to keep in mind that "democracy" here means modern *large-scale* democracy (polyarchy). That a very high degree of democracy can exist in small societies with collective or communal ownership, production, and distribution and virtually no *internal* markets, is shown by the *kibbutzim* of Israel and other very small-scale communist or cooperative societies. Although the *kibbutzim* require conditions that are likely to remain extremely rare, their success and durability invite caution in making generalizations of universal applicability about the absolute essentiality of markets and private property in *every* truly democratic system.

2. Joseph A. Schumpeter, *Capitalism, Socialism and Democracy*, 3rd ed. (New York: Harper and Row, 1950), 167. Characteristically, Schumpeter introduces his doubts at the end of his discussion of socialism and democracy, where he writes that "the task of keeping the democratic course may prove to be extremely delicate. . . . [T]he individuals at the helm . . . might be driven into a course of action which must always have some temptation for men beholding the tremendous power over the people inherent in the socialist organization. After all, effective management of the socialist economy means dictatorship not *of* but *over* the proletariat of the factory. . . . As a matter of practical necessity, socialist democracy may eventually turn out to be more of a sham than capitalist democracy ever was" (p. 302).

3. The attempt at the turn of the century by the American economist J.B. Clark to demonstrate that the distribution of income resulting from competitive markets is also normatively just was quickly rejected and abandoned by other economists, who have adopted the view that the distribution of income is a given from which the validity of their analysis begins. See Marc Blaug, *Economic Theory in Retrospect*, 3rd ed. (New York: Cambridge University Press, 1978), 450ff. For a critique from the standpoint of political theory, see Ian Shapiro, "Three Fallacies Concerning Majorities, Minorities, and Democratic Politics," *NOMOS* XXXII, *Majorities and Minorities* (New York: New York University Press, 1991).

4. For a discussion of some desirable and undesirable solutions to inequalities in incomes and other crucial resources, see James Tobin, "On Limiting the Domain of Inequality," *Journal of Law and Economics* 13 (October 1970): 263-77.

5. One might ask, what larger entity? Humankind? If not humankind, why any smaller aggregation? Although the problem of what aggregate of people is to be taken as relevant in determining an optimal outcome seems to me to pose a neglected question of central importance, I am going to follow the usual (if lamentable) practice of ignoring it here.

6. The most recent effort to estimate the costs and gains in the United States is Robert W. Hahn and John A. Hird, "The Costs and Benefits of Regulation: Review and Synthesis," *Yale Journal on Regulation* 8 (1991): 233-78. Their estimate of the annual costs for 1988 of regulating international trade, telecommunications, agricultural prices, airlines, railroads, postal rates, milk marketing, natural gas, barges, and a half-dozen other activities amounted to $45.3 to 46.5 billion in efficiency costs and $172.2 to 209.5 billion in transfer payments (Table 1, p. 251). They estimate the 1988 costs of social regulation of the environment, highway safety, occupational safety and health, nuclear power, drugs, equal employment opportunities, and consumer product safety as being in the range of $78 to 107 billion, and the benefits $42 to 182 billion. (Table 2, p. 256). "Unlike economic regulation," they note, "where the benefits are thought to be negligible in most cases, social regulation has the potential to confer significant benefits. Because social regulation can address specific 'market failures,' it may provide net benefits to society" (p. 253).

7. I have done so in *Democracy and Its Critics* (New Haven: Yale University Press, 1989).

8. See, for example, John R. Freeman, *Democracies and Markets: The Politics of Mixed Economies* (Ithaca: Cornell University Press, 1989). Even the Scandinavian countries have followed markedly different paths in economic policy making. For example, the "three Nordic countries have developed very different mechanisms for political control of the business cycle. The Norwegian social democrats have primarily emphasized planning with

credit control and, lately, government purchase of industrial stock. The Swedes have relied primarily on labor market control but after the 1960s they also began to promote a more active role in investment. Finally, the Danish social democrats have failed to institute public direction and control of finance, labor market, or investment behavior. In all three countries—but especially in Norway and Denmark—government intervention in income determination assumed major proportions during the 1970s." Gosta Esping-Anderson, *Politics Against Markets* (Princeton: Princeton University Press, 1985), 236-37.

9. The famous "Swedish model" provides an illuminating example. After having developed gradually during a half-century of predominantly Social Democratic governments, its major elements were often seen in Sweden and elsewhere as virtually unalterable components of a fundamental social compact. However, voter dissatisfaction in the 1980s led to a scaling down of income tax rates (to a maximum of 50 percent), and in September 1991 produced the worst electoral defeat for the Social Democratic Party since the 1920s. As a consequence, the nonsocialist parties formed a government and are likely to introduce further, if gradual, changes in some key policies.

9.
THE FUTURE OF SOCIALISM

Francisco C. Weffort

Francisco C. Weffort *is professor of political science at the University of São Paulo in Brazil and a researcher at the Center for Studies of Contemporary Culture (CEDEC), of which he was the founder and first president. He spent the past academic year as a fellow at the Woodrow Wilson Center in Washington. His publications include* América Latina: Ensayos de Interpretación Sociológico-Política *(edited with Fernando Henrique Cardoso, 1970),* O Populismo na Politica Brasiliera *(1978), and* Por que Democracia? *(1986).*

The events of the last three years have hit the left like an earthquake. The collapse of socialism that began in 1989 surprised everyone. It was like a bolt of lightning from a blue sky. Even more shocking were the events of 1991, when the entire Soviet empire unraveled and the Russian Revolution, one of the largest mass movements of modern history, reached its end as an immense and tragic failure. The left everywhere is now facing the most serious challenge in its history.

When Joseph Schumpeter published his classic *Capitalism, Socialism and Democracy* in 1942, it was capitalism that seemed to be doomed. The Great Depression of the 1930s had been followed immediately by the Second World War; fascism, which had scored a string of impressive political successes during the preceding decade, was still cresting toward its military high-water mark. Despite capitalism's tentative recovery in the United States in the late 1930s, it continued to teeter on the brink of collapse in Europe. Allied with Stalin's USSR, the capitalist democracies of the West might win the war (as they did), but even that victory, many thought, would not be enough to save them from ultimate disaster. Since the end of the First World War, socialism had appeared fated to triumph in the modern age. Indeed, even though the march to socialism began to lose strength in the second half of the twentieth century, the socialist mystique endured right up until the fall of the Berlin Wall in 1989.

While he himself loathed socialism, Schumpeter believed that

capitalism would succumb before it. Soviet-style central planning and
state control of production looked to him like the wave of the future.
Perhaps precisely because he was a thoughtful foe of socialism,
Schumpeter provides a striking example of the persuasive force of the
ideologies of his time, and of the tricks that history can play on those
who seek to rely purely on reason. What has been falsified in
Schumpeter's case is not just a particular prediction of socialist victory,
but an entire teleological conception of history, a conception that was not
his alone.

Although it is commonly associated with leftist thought, the idea that
history moves toward a finality long predates the writings of Karl Marx
or the rise of modern socialist groups. Schumpeter puts it forward with
an academic's habitual caution: in the inevitable journey from capitalism
to socialism, he says, one cannot exclude the possibility of chaotic
situations occurring along the way. Schumpeter hedges quite a bit, for
example, when he says that the crucial word "inevitability" refers only
to "tendencies present in an observable pattern" that "never tell us what
will happen . . . but only what *would* happen if they continued to act as
they have been acting in the time interval covered by our observation
and if no other factors intruded."[1] I do not believe that Marx would
disagree with any of this, for though he often spoke as a prophet, he still
enjoyed taking all the precautions of a scientist.

One of the virtues of great and unexpected events like those of 1989-
91 is that they breathe new life into the old idea that history, in the last
analysis, is the history of liberty. The determinism so common among
modern thinkers—be they socialist, liberal, neoconservative, or what have
you—is thus bracingly placed in question. Even when we consider
Schumpeter's efforts to criticize Marx, their commonly held view of
history as necessary movement remains unmistakable in the background.
Schumpeter's prediction, more sociological than economic, that capitalism
would founder due to flagging technological innovation was not
confirmed. And even though modern capitalism has destroyed the
"protecting strata" (craft guilds, aristocratic classes, etc.) just as
Schumpeter feared, this has not had the catastrophic consequences that
he imagined. On the contrary, successful modern capitalism rose to the
challenge by devising other protective mechanisms. In the same way,
capitalism proved itself able to neutralize the hostility of intellectuals,
even to the point of gaining the adherence of many of them.

If the case of Schumpeter is interesting because it suggests that the
intellectual crisis unveiled by the collapse of socialism is not a crisis for
the left alone, Latin America is an interesting region because it is living
proof that the ideological consequences of the events of 1989-91 are not
limited to countries that have experienced "actually existing socialism."
It is known that in the countries of Eastern Europe, the debacle of
socialism was adumbrated by a number of persistent economic failures

and by a slow process of internal ideological corrosion. In Latin America, socialist ideology was kept intact largely through lack of use. With the evident exceptions of Cuba and Chile (which has socialist and communist movements with substantial social roots), Latin American socialism is less a political than an intellectual phenomenon, albeit one with considerable practical importance.

Latin America has traditionally been a happy hunting ground for populist politicians. More recently, political space in different parties has opened up for social democrats, as well as for the expansion of a socially conscious liberalism. These kinds of politics, without being socialist, nonetheless testify to the ideological influence of socialism. Because Latin American capitalism is not famous for its successes or the boldness of its ideological apologists, socialists have an importance in the region's political culture that far exceeds their small numbers. Now, after finding themselves as taken aback as anyone else by the temblors of 1989-91, Latin America's socialists are asking how they can help plan for the reconstruction of their own backward, corporatist, and excessively bureaucratic societies, most of which are stagnating and some of which are disintegrating.

The events of 1989-91 were, strictly speaking, unthinkable in terms of any existing historical paradigm. Perhaps certain teleological and determinist modes of thought had already been in crisis for some time, but the final reserves of leftist confidence in the inexorability of "progress" were maintained until the socialist regimes of Eastern Europe breathed their last. Until 1989, few believed that the socialist countries could ever revert to the social, economic, and political forms characteristic of capitalism. In 1991, the final hopes of the old modes of thought were buried.

The thinking most affected is that associated with Marx, but the consequences go much further. The epochal events of 1989-91 heralded a rediscovery of politics that should shake up not only leftists who put too much stock in deterministic theories of history, but also the many neoconservative apologists for capitalism who affirm the primacy of economic explanations.

The Neoconservative Challenge

All this raises an unavoidable question: What is the meaning of the current epoch? This is obviously too large a topic for the limits of a short essay, but I can propose some hypotheses. I believe that our era is not only one in which confidence in the state has declined while reliance on market mechanisms has risen, but also one in which political democracy and civil society are growing stronger. This point is essential, for it shows that, contrary to what neoconservatives suggest, the market is not the only game in town these days. If socialist thought is to endure and be of relevance, it must begin seriously exploring the significance of hypotheses such as this one.

Schumpeter is important here because of his proposal to replace the classical notion of democracy as an instrument for accomplishing the common good with a newer concept of democracy as an ensemble of procedures for selecting a government by means of peaceful competition between elites. Democracy would then be not so much "government of the people, by the people, for the people" as government by the leaders that the people choose in free elections. Schumpeter implies, moreover, that only a very happy concatenation of circumstances could ever change this into what Lincoln called government "for the people."

I confess that I have mixed feelings whenever I reread Schumpeter's famous chapters concerning democracy. They exude an enormous and unsettling skepticism concerning the rationalism and individualism that are so congenial to the modern mind. On the other hand, Schumpeter's fearless realism establishes a firm basis for grasping the truly autonomous character of political phenomena in the modern world. Furthermore, although he himself explicitly rejected any notion of democracy as an end in itself, he also opened up the possibility of a new point of departure for political analysis that allows his reader to bypass this rejection in favor of any one of a number of routes toward a reconstructed notion of democracy as a value in itself.

The historical experience of recent decades has confirmed for many the view that even procedural democracy cannot be reduced to a question of mere formal rules. In truth, successful democratic procedures presuppose such undeniably substantial things as the institutional arrangements under which people can be free. Without taking things like this into account, how can we hope to understand the global spread of political democracy reflected in the events of 1989-91? Certainly the experiences of democratization in Latin America and in Eastern and Southern Europe should draw our attention to the important distinction between economic systems and cultural values. What is more, they confirm the need to construct theoretical perspectives that avoid any kind of determinism.

Neoconservatives have cast doubt upon the possibility of democratic socialism by defining democracy as if it depended solely on the market economy. The questions that they have raised are good ones, and deserve to be confronted here. Is political liberty possible without economic liberty? My answer is no. Is political democracy possible without the market? My answer again is no. But both these questions and their answers are too abstract to be of much practical use. They were useful in criticizing the totalitarian regimes of Eastern Europe and the former USSR, but they were of very little help in struggles against the "bureaucratic-authoritarian" regimes that flourished until recently in Latin America and Southern Europe. These regimes combined hostility to democracy with state interventionism designed to foster economic development on the capitalist bases of private property and markets.

Under totalitarianism, where the state by definition seeks to exert complete control over economic activity, everything becomes politicized and the economy as such disappears. The distinction between state and society vanishes too, as do the intermediate associations that come between the central government and the individual, and whose importance Tocqueville emphasized. When the state ruthlessly invades society and the economy in this fashion, the liberties of individuals cannot long survive. Neoconservatives thus have a point when they argue that political liberty is not possible without economic liberty, nor democracy without the market.

When they have to deal with the complexity of actual historical conditions, however, the neoconservatives run into difficulties. One of them is that in the formation of totalitarian systems, the state's takeover of the economy does not precede the suppression of political democracy, but follows it. The assertion of state control over the economy is often an eminently political step, taken in order to prepare for war or more effectively wage a war *already* in progress. It is therefore only after an already undemocratic regime has seized the economy that one can speak of this state-controlled economy as a bulwark of the totalitarian regime.

Likewise, the old questions posed by the neoconservatives can do nothing to affect the objections that workers and socialists have long raised against capitalist notions of economic liberty. Are unorganized individual workers economically free in relation to the large firms that employ them? All of the trade unions in all of the democracies of the modern world say no. But if the worker is not free as an individual vis-à-vis the firm, this means that his economic liberty depends less on the market and more on the methods of redress and peaceful self-protection available to him through civil society and democratic politics. Applying the same logic to a different context, we might ask whether the poor are politically free in societies where extreme economic and social inequalities are pervasive facts of life. Anyone who has bothered to review the history of political ideas knows that this last question has hardly been posed only by socialists, but has also been a recurrent theme of political liberalism (even if it is one that neoconservatives would prefer to forget).

Economic Systems and Cultural Values

The questions that the neoconservatives do ask, however, certainly have their uses, the chief of which is to stress the necessity of taking a stand on the theoretical question, "What is liberty?" From what I have said above, it should be clear that I prefer theorists for whom liberty is defined with reference to the sphere of politics. For most neoconservatives, on the other hand, liberty is defined in terms of the economy. Friedrich Hayek, for example, explains the relationship between economic liberty and political liberty in terms that make clear his conviction that the former is primary: "Freedom under the law implies economic freedom, while economic control, as the control of the means for all purposes, makes a restriction of all freedom possible."[2] Hayek rejects the distinction between economic liberalism and political liberalism, and thus reduces political democracy to an instrument of the market. Any possible intervention by the state in the market (with the exception of some services) is a step toward authoritarianism or even totalitarianism. But something rings false in this argument: strictly speaking, Hayek resolves the problem of the relation between economic liberty and political liberty by a definitional procedure. It is as if he has said to the reader: "Take it or leave it." But such an approach to the problem abstracts from its historical character.

Hannah Arendt takes up the same question but handles it in a different way, leaving it open so that it may be resolved through reflection on (and participation in) history. Heiress of a tradition that goes back to Tocqueville, Arendt makes even more use than her predecessors did of themes drawn from classical antiquity: the realm of economics (in its original sense of private or family life, which in antiquity included slavery) is the kingdom of necessity; liberty can only appear in the public arena of political activity.[3]

Arendt would probably agree with Hayek in warning of the danger of authoritarianism that can arise when the "social question" makes its way into the political sphere. But unlike the neoconservatives, she rejects any sort of economic determinism. And in spite of occasional (and understandable) relapses into various forms of pessimism concerning the prospects for liberty in the modern world, she finally came to believe that people have an opportunity to become free in and through political action—"by their words and deeds," as she put it. Arendt interprets the revolutions of the modern era, for example, in a way that no determinist (whether Marxist or neoconservative) could accept when she claims that at their base lies the struggle of liberty against tyranny.[4] Could there be a more original—or in hindsight, more obvious—assessment of the events of 1989-91?

In this, the hour of their deepest perplexity, socialists might do well to consult Norberto Bobbio's essay *Which Socialism?*[5] In his suggestively titled work, Bobbio summed up the quandary of democratic socialism by noting that no democratic country had arrived at socialism, and no socialist country had arrived at democracy. Bobbio, himself a "liberal socialist," was implying what we all now know: to attain democracy, the countries of Eastern Europe would have to abandon socialism. As I suggested above, there is no way to deny that this means a clear political victory for neoconservatism. Totalitarian socialism, in which the socialization of production is understood to mean state control of production, leads to political oppression and economic stagnation. Thus the will to liberty that flourishes in a resurgent civil society turns necessarily against the state, demanding a transition to democracy and capitalism. After the world has witnessed this turn of events in Eastern Europe, socialists can survive as a political force only by finding a whole new *raison d'être*.

With state socialism having fallen, socialists now find themselves groping to explain to themselves and others just what a serious socialist alternative to capitalism would look like. Yet if the distinction between economic systems and cultural values that I suggested above makes sense, socialists can feel as confident as ever about old socialist values like equality, social justice, and so on. It is this "cultural" dimension of socialism that explains why there are still so many socialists in the world. Although some might say that these values are widely accepted within modern democracies and are therefore not specifically socialist, this should not be seen as a serious objection. We are talking precisely about *democratic* socialism. Thus it will not be surprising if socialists, given their lack of alternative economic and social theories, embrace in the coming years a conception of socialism that is not bound up with a particular system but is defined primarily in terms of values.

State and Market

Eduard Bernstein said long ago that "the movement is everything, the end is nothing." In the heroic days of social democracy, the "movement" was a struggle by workers and social democrats to realize concrete demands within capitalist society, while the "end" was the idea of a socialist society that would replace capitalism and eliminate exploitation. Today, however, our experience with modern democracies in general and modern social democracies in particular allows us to say a little more. Bernstein was right in claiming that the "movement" is more important than the "end," simply because it is the movement that leads the way to—and in that sense creates—the end. In history there are no already marked paths, for as the saying goes, "what makes the beaten track is walking."

When Bernstein asserted that the end is nothing, however, he was indulging in a polemical exaggeration that should not be taken literally. The end is surely no longer the *certain* appearance of a future socialist society that is destined to arise necessarily out of the internal contradictions of capitalism. That is how Bernstein's "antirevisionist" foes in the socialist movement of the late nineteenth and early twentieth centuries conceived of the "end." In an era like ours, with its manifold uncertainties, socialists should be the last ones to become preoccupied with revindicating old certainties. But how can socialism dispense with a goal to pursue? In truth, the end exists, but as a free project, not a fated outcome; it may be accomplished only partially, or even frustrated by great obstacles and unforeseen events. Furthermore, while the end is a vision of the future, it must change according to the circumstances of the present. It is a project inspired by high ideals, but it is not everything. It has no guarantee of certainty, despite what the followers of "scientific socialism" thought, but it is something significant. It is the intention of the walker, without which the journey would not have meaning and would probably never have been undertaken.

If a socialist perspective on the future is still possible, it must come from the vantage point that the events of 1989-91 have afforded us as we contemplate the history of democracy in our time. In Eastern Europe, Southern Europe, and Latin America, the state was defeated in its efforts to control the economy and society. The state had been on the offensive since at least the First World War in a variety of economic and political settings. Socialist and fascist variants of totalitarianism, "bureaucratic-authoritarian" regimes, and a cluster of other authoritarianisms are the most conspicuous—but not the only—political forms that have led the state on its drive to expand throughout the years. The massive growth of the state in our century has not been confined to dictatorships, however, but has touched all modern democracies as well.

A democratic socialist perspective should have room for the market, but it should also embrace political democracy and the development of civil society, and incorporate social, ideological, and institutional pluralism.[6] The central problem for socialism today is to show that societies can achieve a form of self-government that combines the principles of social equality with those of political liberty. Democratic socialism derives its inspiration from a radical conception of democracy. This does not mean that it seeks the impossible goal of eliminating all differences between rulers and ruled, but rather that it seeks always to improve the institutions of political democracy and civil society, especially those that are tied to the world of work. Such a perspective does not and cannot exclude the recognition that the most advanced sectors of the economy are more and more transnational or even global in character. To reject this internationalization is to accept backwardness and stagnation.

Yet even in the most advanced modern society, no market functions automatically. In the best of cases, the healthy functioning of the market is guaranteed, stimulated, even driven by social and political institutions and by administrative rules written and enforced by the state, as John Kenneth Galbraith demonstrated for the case of the United States.[7] It is true that states frequently disturb markets, but no one has yet found a way to make markets work without some state involvement. The recognition of this fact of life of modern democracies does not imply any effort to restore state socialism; rather, it is a bit of simple realism that imposes itself on anyone who is familiar with modern history. (As for state socialism, while it has not yet died out entirely as a reality—it lives on in places like China and Cuba, for instance—it has definitely perished as an ideological model.)

From this perspective, the ideological tendency of many neoconservatives to understand the relationship between state and market in polarizing terms leads to the odd conclusion that no really existing society can consider itself a market economy. All democratic societies—which are what interest us here—have mixed economies in which economic activities are divided between state and market in diverse ways. As examples we could cite the interventionist state in Japan, the social democracies of Germany and Sweden, or the liberal democracies of England and the United States.

The rich historical experience that modern democracies have had with mixed economies can teach us many things. In the first place, it shows that some state presence, even a prominent presence, in the economy does not by itself lead to authoritarianism or totalitarianism. Modern democratic society is not a society of the "minimal state," but on the contrary presupposes a strong state; at the same time, it also requires that civil society and democracy be strong enough to control the state. There is a permanent tension between the state and the market, but each needs the other. No modern democracy can either do without the market, as less thoughtful socialists claim, or get by with a "minimal state" of the sort that neoconservatives idealize.

Lessons for Socialists

For democratic socialists, however, the greatest lesson is another. If neoconservative thinking tends toward determinism and the monism of the market, democratic socialist thinking has to be pluralistic and open to many possibilities. Socialist interpretations ought always to consider the social order as a plural reality of which the state, the market, democratic political culture, and autonomous civil society all form basic elements. The hallmark that distinguishes socialist movements from other democratic political forces is their overriding concern with stimulating society to achieve greater equality and greater liberty. In an era in which the capitalist economy is increasingly a worldwide phenomenon, socialists must learn to live with the most advanced forms of capitalism if they want to keep their feet on the ground and move toward modernity. But they need not be identified, in their values or their movements, with the "soul" of capitalism. Socialists should marry democracy out of love, but their union with the market need be no more than a "marriage of convenience."[8]

Will this put them in a more fragile position than those earlier socialists who, as Schumpeter has so well described, believed in a supposedly "scientific" socialism and thought that "historical necessity" was on their side? I do not think so. But even if their new position does turn out to be weaker, that will be the minimal price that every socialist who really values democracy as an end in itself will have to pay. You can only be a democrat if you plainly see and acknowledge from the outset that your own point of view is a partial one, not that of everyone or of society as a whole. If socialism achieves a new meaning and makes a corresponding political comeback, it will be because socialists have learned, finally, to accept the presence of their adversaries as legitimate players in the democratic game. That will require the admission that socialism, in any imaginable form, should be understood as a *possibility* rather than as a historical *necessity*. After the events of 1989-91, it should be easy for socialists, of all people, to see that they are not the masters of the future.

By the same token, it should also be easy for them to understand the grave mistake of those who, through a curious ideological inversion, have come to imagine that the masters of the future are the capitalists. If history, as Lord Acton said, is the history of liberty, then the future simply does not have a master. This is the most promising of the many lessons that are to be gleaned from the events of 1989-91, and it must be learned by all who wish to help build societies that are freer, more modern, and—if the left can fulfill its task—more equal.

NOTES

1. Joseph A. Schumpeter, *Capitalism, Socialism and Democracy*, 3rd ed. (New York: Harper and Row, 1950), 61. Emphasis in original.

2. Friedrich Hayek, "Liberalism," in *New Studies in Philosophy, Politics, Economics, and the History of Ideas* (Chicago: University of Chicago Press, 1978), 132.

3. Hannah Arendt, *The Human Condition* (Chicago: University of Chicago Press, 1958), Part VI: "The Vita Activa and the Modern Age."

4. Arendt, *On Revolution* (New York: Viking Press, 1963).

5. Norberto Bobbio, *Which Socialism?* trans. Roger Griffin (Minneapolis: University of Minnesota Press, 1987).

6. This only sketches a theoretical program which, unfortunately, I do not have the space to describe fully here. Important suggestions can be found in Alec Nove, *The Economics of Feasible Socialism* (London: George Allen and Unwin, 1983), Part V: "Feasible Socialism." Also very suggestive is the essay by Alan Wolfe, "Three Ways for Development: Market, State, and Civil Society" (unpublished manuscript, New School for Social Research, August 1991).

7. John Kenneth Galbraith, *The New Industrial State* (Boston: Houghton-Mifflin, 1967).

8. This idea was suggested to me, in a slightly different context, by Professor Jeffrey Weintraub of the University of California, San Diego. Letter to author.

10.
CAPITALISM & DEMOCRACY: THE MISSING LINK

Francis Fukuyama

Francis Fukuyama *is a resident consultant to the RAND Corporation in Washington, D.C. He has previously been deputy director of the U.S. State Department's policy planning staff, a senior staff member in the political science department at RAND, and a graduate fellow at the Center for Science and International Affairs at Harvard University. His 1989 article "The End of History?" has been translated into many languages and has become the subject of controversy around the world. He has just published a fuller exposition of his views on this theme in* The End of History and the Last Man *(Free Press, 1992).*

The past half-century has seen a remarkable inversion of the expectations that Joseph Schumpeter expressed in his *Capitalism, Socialism and Democracy*. Rather than capitalism leading inevitably to socialism, as he predicted, socialism has inexorably given way to capitalism. Meanwhile, capitalism and democracy—which he believed to be strongly at odds—have found a way of coexisting, indeed, of reinforcing one another. The reasons for these dramatic reversals of Schumpeter's expectations can be found in two developments: first, the changing character of the industrialization process driven by modern natural science; and second, a growing consensus concerning the legitimacy of liberal democracy in an autonomous realm of politics.

Despite socialism's current poor reputation, it is clear in retrospect that it formed a perfectly viable economic alternative to capitalism in the early phases of industrialization. The Soviet Union's GNP grew at a rate of 4.4 to 6.6 percent per year between 1928 and 1955—a remarkable figure given the havoc and destruction wreaked first by Stalin's forced collectivization and then by World War II—and at a rate half again as fast as the United States in the two decades from 1955 to 1975.[1] These figures may have to be revised once the many hidden costs of Soviet-style industrialization are taken into account, such as environmental damage and intangible but seriously deleterious effects on the work ethic.

Still it remains true that the USSR succeeded in transforming itself into an industrial giant in less than a generation without allowing much in the way of either political or economic freedom. At one time, it seemed that this type of state-directed industrialization from above was the *only* way of producing such rapid results, though the experience of much of East Asia would suggest the existence of a kinder and gentler approach based on markets. But the Soviet achievement cannot be denied, or dismissed as a route to a certain stage of industrial modernity.

It is clear too that this early phase of industrialization had many similar social consequences, whether it occurred under socialism or capitalism. That is, peasants were drawn or pushed out of the countryside and into large industrial cities; traditional social groups and forms of authority were replaced by "modern" rational and bureaucratic ones; and overall levels of education, both mass and elite, increased substantially.[2] Thus socialist development, in a sense, created the social basis for the eventual breakdown of communist totalitarianism by creating an educated and relatively cosmopolitan urban class, the class that produced Gorbachev and those who supported him in the late 1980s.

But while socialism was able to produce the level of industrialization represented by the American midwestern "rust belt"—steel, chemicals, tractors, and the like—its failure as an economic system lay in its inability to achieve subsequent levels of industrial modernity. In predicting that socialism would ultimately replace capitalism, Schumpeter failed to anticipate the emergence of what has been variously labeled "postindustrial society," the "information age," the "technetronic era," and so forth. Economic life in the second half of the twentieth century came to be far more complex and information-intensive, oriented toward services rather than manufacturing, and dependent on dizzying rates of technological innovation to maintain productivity gains and growth. Under these circumstances, central planning and centralized economic decision making became increasingly inefficient. Since Schumpeter wrote *Capitalism, Socialism and Democracy* less than a decade after the world had passed through the trough of the Great Depression, at the point of transition between the old and new economic eras, his mistake is quite understandable, but a mistake it nonetheless was.

Schumpeter clearly underestimated capitalism's vitality and ability to adjust to these new circumstances. Based on historical performance, Schumpeter predicted overall growth in the capitalist world of 2 percent for the period 1928-78; actual performance for the OECD world for this period was double that, and individual countries like Japan and Taiwan managed to achieve rates of GNP growth of 10 percent and higher for extended periods of time. Many of the negative consequences of capitalist development, moreover, either failed to materialize, or else turned out to be much less decisive than he had believed.

For example, much of Schumpeter's critique of capitalism was based on what he believed to be the increasingly oligopolistic nature of competition. This assumption was based, in turn, on the idea that technology dictated an ever-increasing optimal size for firms.[3] In practice, however, technology did not always favor large firms: in many industries, from computers to retailing, there were clear diseconomies of scale that promoted smaller firms, new market entrants, and increasing levels of competition. Nor was there a "routinization" of entrepreneurship, as Schumpeter feared (p. 132), since advancing technology opened up enormous new areas of opportunity for risk-taking individuals. Finally and perhaps most importantly, capitalism did not dig its own grave by producing an intellectual class unalterably opposed to it. According to Schumpeter:

> [T]he capitalist process produced [an] atmosphere of almost universal hostility to its own social order. . . . The capitalist process . . . eventually decreases the importance of the function by which the capitalist class lives. . . . [C]apitalism creates a critical frame of mind which, after having destroyed the moral authority of so many other institutions, in the end turns against its own; the bourgeois finds to his amazement that the rationalist attitude does not stop at the credentials of kings and popes but goes on to attack private property and the whole scheme of bourgeois values (p. 143).

While the anticapitalist biases of intellectuals have remained strong and remarkably persistent, the sheer productivity of capitalist economies succeeded over time in coopting significant numbers of them, to the point where, by the 1980s, many of the most incisive critical minds in Europe and America were busy dissecting the failings of socialism instead of capitalism.

Some of Schumpeter's predictions about capitalism did prove true. The divorce between management and ownership is an issue that continues to figure in contemporary American debates about competitiveness, for example, and everyone has had to live with the consequences of the breakdown of the bourgeois family (p. 157). But in general, such "contradictions" indirectly engendered by capitalism failed to delegitimize it as an economic system in the 50 years after Schumpeter wrote.

Misreading Socialism

At the same time, Schumpeter did not anticipate several key weaknesses of socialism in the new environment created by postindustrial society. In the first place, Schumpeter asserts that central planning ministries of the future will simply direct enterprises to "produce as economically as possible," an injunction that becomes more critical in an era of accelerating technological change (p. 175). But he failed to specify what incentives would lead enterprise directors to economize on resources or incorporate new technology. The experience of the Soviet Union indicates that the application of new technology is every bit as dependent on personal monetary incentives as is labor on the factory floor.

Second, Schumpeter dismisses the argument, advanced most forcefully by "Austrian school" economists like Friedrich Hayek and Ludwig von Mises, that planning boards face tasks of "unmanageable complication." In fact, the "Austrians" were right: the sheer complexity of modern economies mandated some form of decentralized economic decision making, which no amount of linear programming or large computers could duplicate. To cite just one example, Goskomtsen, the pricing bureau of the former Soviet Union, set about 200,000 prices each year, or 42 percent of all administered prices in the former USSR.[4] This might have been adequate for the number of commodities produced by a European country in the 1920s, but today, a single airliner can be composed of well over a million different parts.[5]

Third, Schumpeter was wrong to assert that socialist industry could be more efficient than its capitalist counterpart because socialism reduced uncertainty in economic decision making. Uncertainty proved to be not a source of inefficiency but rather the necessary result of the process of evaluation of production possibilities and market opportunities in a dynamic, technologically driven economic environment. The certainties of enterprise managers in actual socialist societies turned out to be symptoms of their inability to innovate or to seek out new markets effectively.

Indeed, many aspects of Schumpeter's picture of a future socialist economy now seem laughable in retrospect. Quite apart from strictly economic questions, Schumpeter was unable to foresee how illegitimate socialism itself would appear to be in the eyes of the very working class that was its declared beneficiary. At one point, in discussing the maintenance of labor discipline in a socialist economy, he notes:

> Economic policy will therefore be rationalized and some of the worst sources of waste will be avoided simply because the economic significance of measures and processes will be patent to every comrade. Among other things, every comrade will realize the true significance of restiveness at work and especially of strikes. It does not matter in the least that he will not on that account *ex post facto* condemn the strikes of the capitalist period, provided he comes to the conclusion that strikes would "now" be nothing else but antisocial attacks upon the nation's welfare. If he struck all the same, he would do so with a bad conscience and meet public disapproval (p. 212).

Much of this sounds rather strange in light of the experience of Solidarity in Poland. Not only was the socialist ideal an insufficient substitute for the profit motive; socialism itself became an object of active hatred for large numbers of people living under it.

Thus capitalism proved to be far more flexible and adaptable than socialism in adjusting to the new economic conditions created by technological change in the second half of the twentieth century. To put it somewhat schematically, in conditions of increasing industrial maturity, capitalism tended to evolve into advanced capitalism, while socialism tended to give way to capitalism, both for purely economic reasons. In retrospect, Walt Rostow's much-maligned characterization of communism as a "disease of the transition [to mature development]" seems quite accurate: however monstrous in other ways, communism was a perfectly adequate *economic* system for making the leap from an agrarian to an urban-industrial society, but it proved itself unable to meet the requirements of postindustrial modernity, and therefore had to be transcended or abolished.[6]

Economic Development and Democracy

If socialism tends to evolve into capitalism in response to the requirements of postindustrial economic modernity, is there a corresponding economic imperative that inclines modernizing societies toward democracy? Here the answer is much less clear. That there is a strong *empirical* correlation between development and democracy is reasonably certain. When Seymour Martin Lipset noted this correlation in 1959, he was criticized on a number of grounds.[7] For example, while relatively more developed states within a given region tended to be more democratic, many of the Latin American democracies that Lipset mentioned were less developed than a number of authoritarian regimes in Europe, on both the left and right. But in the 30 years since Lipset wrote, many of these anomalies have been corrected. The states of Southern Europe have both democratized and developed economically, while a large bloc of developed communist dictatorships in Eastern Europe have democratized since the fall of the Berlin Wall in 1989. The correlation was weakened somewhat by the democratization in this period of a number of very poor Third World countries like Peru and the Philippines, and by the rapid economic growth of a number of authoritarian countries like Singapore and Thailand. There are also certain states in the Middle East—Kuwait, Saudi Arabia, and the United Arab Emirates—that have per capita incomes on a par with Europe or North America but are not democratic; this anomaly is easily explained, however, by the accident of their location on top of the world's largest reserves of crude oil.

Nonetheless, there are in 1992 virtually no examples of highly industrialized countries that are not stable democracies, and very few extremely poor countries that are. Moreover, many countries that have experienced democratic revolutions in the past generation, including Spain, Portugal, Greece, Brazil, South Korea, Taiwan, the Afrikaner community in South Africa, and the Soviet Union, all made the transition from being predominantly agricultural countries at midcentury to being industrialized, urbanized ones at the time of democratization.[8]

More interesting than the mere existence of this correlation is the reason for it. In particular, it is worth asking whether there is any *economically* necessary reason why advanced industrialization should lead to democracy as it does to capitalism. Some have argued that democracy is more functional in reconciling interests in a complex modern economy.[9] Many other observers stress the importance of education in fostering democracy. Yet while education is unquestionably helpful in sustaining democracy, it is not at all clear that education per se inclines people to choose democracy over other possible forms of government. An engineering student from South Korea studying in an American university may pick up democratic ideas while in the United States, but these will be incidental to the educational goals determined by South Korea's economic needs; had a comparable student studied in Berlin in 1935, he might well have returned home with fascist ideas. For many years, some of the most educated and cultured people in Europe and America were ardent believers in Stalinism, or at any rate in some form of nondemocratic socialism; it was their less educated peers who provided the bedrock support for liberal democracy.

It is possible to short-circuit much of this debate on the economic necessity of democracy simply by pointing out that many of the most impressive economic growth records in the last 150 years have been compiled not by democracies, but by authoritarian states with more or less capitalist economic systems. This was true of both Meiji Japan and the German Second Reich in the latter half of the nineteenth century, as well as any number of more recent modernizing authoritarian regimes such as Franco's Spain, post-1953 South Korea, Taiwan, Brazil, Singapore, or Thailand.[10]

Apart from empirical evidence on this score, there is good reason to think that democracies as a whole should not be particularly efficient economically, or at least not as efficient as competent authoritarian regimes that make economic growth their chief priority. Democracies tend to transfer wealth from rich to poor in the interests of social equality, to protect or subsidize failing industries, to spend more on social services than investment, and the like. The military regime in South Korea accelerated economic growth by suppressing strikes and holding down wages and consumption; the transition to democracy in 1987 led to a wave of labor unrest and rapidly rising wages that ultimately reduced Korea's international competitiveness. To take an example closer to home, the United States has amassed a massive budget deficit over the past decade, about whose pernicious effects there is universal agreement; American democracy, however, has not been able to eliminate it because of an inability to agree on how to apportion the pain of either spending cuts or tax increases.

Of course, there is no guarantee that authoritarian states will make rational economic choices. While a military government ruled during Brazil's period of rapid economic growth between 1964 and 1972, it was another military government that created the Brazilian debt crisis of the late 1970s. But in theory, a competent authoritarian government that makes economic growth its top priority should be able to achieve this goal more easily than a liberal democracy, as many countries in Asia have shown.

Communism was, arguably, overthrown in Eastern Europe and the former Soviet Union because people wanted capitalist abundance. In countries like Spain and South Korea, however, the choice of prosperity without liberty was available, yet democratic revolutions occurred anyway. The reasons why economic development fosters democracy must therefore be found outside the realm of economics. The choice of democracy must spring from the realm of politics and ideology—that is, from man's self-conscious effort to think through his situation in society and to devise rules and institutions that are in some manner in accord with his underlying nature. The realm of politics has its own autonomous ends, and therefore cannot be comprehensively explained according to the subpolitical categories of economics or sociology. While certain ideologies are better fostered under certain specific social and economic circumstances, they must first be understood in their own terms.

The Desire for Recognition

I have elsewhere argued that the chief psychological imperative underlying democracy is the desire for universal and equal recognition.[11] That is, all authoritarian regimes, including dictatorships of the left based on the principle of equality, are versions of the master-slave relationship in which the dignity of certain "masters" (the "ruling elite," "master race," "vanguard party," or what have you) is "recognized," whereas that of the great mass of citizens is not. The desire for recognition is a completely noneconomic source of motivation that can take a wide variety of forms, and it is in certain ways also the basis for nondemocratic alternatives like theocracy or aggressive nationalism. But only liberal democracy can *rationally* satisfy the human desire for recognition, through the granting of the elementary rights of citizenship on a universal and equal basis.

The principle of universal recognition originated historically in the Christian doctrine of the universal equality of man before God, which explains the high degree of correlation between stable democracy and Christian culture in the world today.[12] But if democracy represents in some way the secularization of certain Christian themes or doctrines, it thereby lays the basis for their potential universalization, much as the scientific method, historically a European invention, has become universally accessible. With the French and American revolutions, the principle of universal recognition was implemented in the world's most advanced countries, and it is this principle which remains the most rational two hundred years later.

The victory of the principle of universal recognition is by no means assured by its superior rationality alone, and in this century it has been locked in mortal combat with the alternatives represented by fascism and communism. But in the end, the massive rejection of communism by populations across Eastern Europe and the former Soviet Union did represent the emergence of a higher rationality in politics. For while those anticommunist revolutions were driven to some degree by the economic crisis of socialism, the totality of the revolutionary phenomena cannot be explained without considering the clearly expressed desire of many of the "democrats" to live in a society of rational recognition—one in which their elementary rights were recognized under a rule of law.

The desire for recognition, then, can provide the missing link between economic development and democracy that economic or functional explanations by themselves do not provide. In preindustrial societies most people are consumed with getting their share of a virtually fixed stock of wealth, or even with sheer physical survival; as society becomes richer and more secure, however, people become free to seek nonmaterial goals like recognition of their status and political participation. That is to say, the slave must be educated slowly and painfully to understand that he or she is a human being with a unique dignity that can best be recognized by certain kinds of social and political institutions. Ideologies like Christianity, democracy, or socialism are all means by which slaves attempt to come to terms with their condition of servitude, and to find a means of satisfying their desire for recognition. While education is no guarantee that liberal democracy will eventually be seen as the best means of securing such recognition, it is at least helpful toward that end, since human beings cannot be led to see the inherent rationality of universal recognition except through a process of education.

There are other reasons for expecting economic modernization to prepare the ground for stable democracy. Dynamic economic growth often tends to promote a certain kind of equality of condition helpful to the long-term stability of democracy. Development—and in particular, capitalist development—of course promotes many kinds of economic inequalities, but these are new and relatively fluid stratifications that cut across old class and status lines, in the process eliminating many traditional and more entrenched sources of inequality. The result is captured in the phrase "middle-class society," which does not imply the elimination of all substantive inequalities; it suggests rather that the most important inequalities will be based not on inherited social position but on education, occupation, and individual achievement. Middle-class societies featuring high social mobility are obviously better environments for fostering liberal democracy than those riven by longstanding class barriers. The latter tend to foster not only authoritarian ideologies upholding an inegalitarian status quo, but also authoritarian ideologies of the left committed to smashing the existing order at all costs.

Economic development is neither a necessary nor a sufficient condition for stable democracy; it is, however, very helpful. There are numerous examples of underdeveloped or agrarian countries that have succeeded in sustaining workable democracies over extended periods of time, such as Costa Rica or India, or the United States itself in its earliest years. Conversely, there are also examples of highly developed countries that have not been democracies, such as Nazi Germany or Japan before 1945. There are no deterministic laws linking development and democracy; development simply creates conditions that are conducive to the acceptance of democratic norms and ideology. Democratization is an autonomous political process, however, that is dependent on a variety of political factors including: the apparent success of democracy relative to its authoritarian competitors in other countries; the fortunes of war (and peace) in the international system; the skill and competence of the individual leaders who seek to create and consolidate democratic systems; and sheer accident. There are also cultural obstacles to stable democracy, such as religion, ethnicity, preexisting social structure, and the like, that are independent of the level of economic development and affect the possibility of democracy. As we will see below, these factors raise questions about how well the relationship between development and democracy will hold up in Asia in the future.

The relationship between capitalism and democracy is an indirect one. That is, capitalism in itself does not generate direct pressures for democracy. It is perfectly compatible with many forms of authoritarianism (though obviously not with communist totalitarianism), and may even flourish better in nondemocracies. But capitalism is a more efficient engine of economic growth than socialism, and thus is more likely to generate the rapid socioeconomic change that favors the emergence of stable democracy.

The Asian Alternative

In Asia, the relationship between economic development and democracy postulated by modernization theory has held up reasonably well.[13] The region's three most economically developed states (leaving aside Australia and New Zealand) are Japan, Taiwan, and South Korea; all have become democracies (or in Taiwan's case, at least more democratic) since 1945 as economic growth has transformed their societies. In 1989, the People's Republic of China also experienced democratic upheaval. The unrest came from the most modern sector of its population, which had benefited from the economic reforms of the early 1980s. In South Korea, one could see how the emergence of a broad, educated, increasingly professional middle class led by the mid-1980s to demands for a political system that, in addition to providing for economic growth, recognized the rights and capacity for self-government of its citizens.

On the other hand, there are grounds for thinking that Asian political development could turn away from democracy and take its own unique path in spite of the region's record of economic growth. Liberal democracy has always been interpreted somewhat differently in Asia than in North America or Europe. Traditional group hierarchies pervade the social structures of all culturally Confucian societies, from Thailand to Japan, despite the formal commitment to democratic universalism and equality in the latter country. Such hierarchies are the basis for an overt form of paternalistic authoritarianism in countries like Singapore. Unlike fundamentalist Islam or communism, this Asian form of "soft" authoritarianism is clearly quite compatible with advanced capitalism and hence the highest levels of technological modernity. Singapore's former premier Lee Kuan Yew would argue that such a political system is much more suited to Confucian cultures than is the chaotic individualism of Western democracy. More than that, an increasing number of Asians would argue that this type of authoritarianism is *superior* to the individualism of Western liberal democracy in producing the highly educated, motivated, and disciplined populations necessary to achieve an advanced, technological, postindustrial society.

It is significant for the ideological future of Asia that such arguments are being voiced to an increasing extent in Japan, which serves as a model for the rest of the region. In the immediate postwar period, most Japanese shared many of the hypotheses of modernization theory, believing that the "traditional" elements of their society and political system, such as the emphasis on group consensus and vertical *sempai-kohai* (patron-protégé) relationships, would erode with the process of economic development. But Japan's remarkable economic success relative to established Western democracies has led to a reevaluation of these traditional elements of culture, and to the belief that they are not embarrassing holdovers from a premodern past, but rather great strengths that form an intrinsic component of the Japanese economic miracle.

Asia thus seems to be at a significant crossroads that will test the validity of the link between development and democracy. On the one hand, it is quite possible to imagine the region sticking to the modernizing trajectory of the last 40 years, in which democracy is the natural outgrowth of advancing industrialization. Group consensus would gradually give way to individualism, manifested in the increasing power of consumers, women, and other nontraditional sectors. On the other hand, politics could take an autonomous turn if Asians come to believe more strongly that continued economic modernization in the "post-postindustrial" world requires a reemphasis on traditional Asian values at the expense of Western democratic norms. It is here, perhaps, that the future relationship between capitalism and democracy will be defined.

NOTES

1. These figures are taken from Ed Hewett, *Reforming the Soviet Economy: Equality versus Efficiency* (Washington, D.C.: Brookings Institution, 1988), 38.

2. For further discussion of Soviet modernization and its political consequences, see Moshe Lewin, *The Gorbachev Phenomenon: A Historical Interpretation* (Berkeley: University of California Press, 1987).

3. Joseph A. Schumpeter, *Capitalism, Socialism and Democracy*, 3rd ed. (New York: Harper and Row, 1950), 189. All subsequent page references to this work are given in the text above.

4. Hewett, op. cit., 192.

5. Moreover, in addition to the multiplication of the number of commodities and services, there is enormous differentiation in the quality of products produced by a modern industrial economy, which central planning boards would be inherently poor at judging.

6. Walt Rostow, *The Stages of Economic Growth: A Non-Communist Manifesto* (Cambridge: Cambridge University Press, 1965), 162-64.

7. Seymour Martin Lipset, "Some Social Requisites of Democracy: Economic Development and Political Legitimacy," *American Political Science Review* 53 (1959): 69-105. See also Phillips Cutright, "National Political Development: Its Measurements and Social Correlates," *American Sociology Review* 28 (1963): 253-64; and Deane E. Neubauer, "Some Conditions of Democracy,"*American Political Science Review* 61 (1967): 1002-9.

8. For a review of the literature that largely confirms this point, see Larry Diamond, "Economic Development and Democracy Reconsidered," *American Behavioral Scientist* 15 (March-June 1992): 450-99.

9. Talcott Parsons, "Evolutionary Universals in Society," *American Sociological Review* 29 (June 1964): 339-57.

10. Between 1961 and 1968, for example, the average annual growth rate of the developing world's democracies, including India, Ceylon, the Philippines, Chile, and Costa Rica, was only 2.1 percent, whereas the group of conservative authoritarian regimes (Spain, Portugal, Iran, Taiwan, South Korea, Thailand, and Pakistan) had an average growth rate of 5.2 percent. See Samuel P. Huntington and Jorge I. Dominguez, "Political Development," in Fred Greenstein and Nelson Polsby, eds., *Handbook of Political Science*, vol. 3 (Reading, Mass.: Addison-Wesley, 1975), 61.

11. See Francis Fukuyama, *The End of History and the Last Man* (New York: Free Press, 1992), especially 143-208.

12. This correlation is noted in Samuel P. Huntington, *The Third Wave: Democratization in the Late Twentieth Century* (Norman, Okla.: University of Oklahoma Press, 1991), 72-85.

13. On this point, see Lucian Pye's presidential address to the American Political Science Association, "Political Science and the Crisis of Authoritarianism," *American Political Science Review* 84 (1990): 3-17; and the introductory chapter to Pye's *Asian Power and Politics: The Cultural Dimensions of Authority* (Cambridge: Harvard University Press, 1985).

11.
THE FUTURE OF AN ILLUSION

Arturo Fontaine Talavera

Arturo Fontaine Talavera *is the director of the Centro de Estudios Públicos (CEP), a prominent public policy research institute in Santiago, Chile. He also serves as editorial director of the institute's quarterly publication,* Estudios Públicos. *He is a professor at the Institute of Political Science of the Catholic University of Chile, where he teaches political philosophy. His novel* Oír su voz *has just been published in Buenos Aires by Editorial Planeta.*

Though there is much with which I agree in the splendid essays by Francisco Weffort and Francis Fukuyama, I want to focus here on certain points in their respective contributions that I find questionable or obscure.

Weffort is concerned with the aims and ideas that will characterize socialism in the future. After the communist debacle of 1989-91, one might well have asked if socialism even has a future. Weffort avoids this question, asking instead what the new meaning of socialism will be after the collapse of communism. After thus assuming without argument that socialism can survive, he tries to stake out its new meaning by setting up certain side constraints: future socialism will be 1) democratic (as opposed to authoritarian or totalitarian), and 2) compatible with private property and the market economy (as opposed to requiring state ownership and central command of the economy).

So far, so good. But given these constraints, what distinguishes democratic socialism from democratic capitalism? Apparently, there will be more state intervention—and hence less room for the market—for the sake of reducing inequalities. There is nothing futuristic about this position, which social democrats and Fabian socialists have been defending for decades. Weffort neither acknowledges this fact nor seeks to answer any of the criticisms that have been raised in the past against this brand of socialism.

The main point to be noted here is less the failure of totalitarian socialism than the drift and confusion that now beset democratic socialism. In Spain, the current socialist government favors free markets much more than the right-wing dictatorship of General Francisco Franco ever did. In other countries, socialism represents a conservative force, closely linked to certain interest groups (e.g., key trade union associations) that resist the changes which are advocated by groups favoring free markets.

Perhaps there is a way out. Perhaps the ideal of equality can be reinterpreted in some powerful new fashion. But to do so in a manner consistent with democracy and competitive markets will surely prove a task of extreme difficulty. Weffort's essay exemplifies this difficulty and does little to assuage my fear that in many countries democratic socialism might mean merely a new type of mercantilism advancing under the banner of equality. Nor do I see any signs of an attractive new socialist agenda. Just compare socialism's fading cultural appeal with the allure of the ecology movement. At least for the time being, socialism has lost its loveliness.

At the heart of socialism—at least of the Latin American variety—lies the belief that the economy ought to answer to the will of the people expressed through political channels. The ideal of a people's cooperative, where each person has an equal vote, is contrasted with the market, where there are huge inequalities of income and power. A contemporary democratic socialist may accept the market as the main allocator of resources, but still favors democratically enacted political interventions designed to correct market results in the name of equality. We all know that such interventions can be and have been carried out without destroying capitalism. We also know that they have certain costs and risks.

Schumpeter pointed out the naivete of the "classical doctrine of democracy," which holds that "the people itself decide[s] issues through the election of individuals who are to assemble in order to carry out its will."[1] Democratic socialists seem never to have learned this lesson, and often act instead as if the "classical doctrine" were true. "Democracy," wrote Schumpeter, "does not mean and cannot mean that the people actually rule in any obvious sense of the terms 'people' and 'rule.' Democracy means only that the people have the opportunity of accepting or refusing the men who are to rule them" (pp. 284-85).

That is why it is so easy even for elected politicians to use the power of the state to secure privileges. An interventionist political agenda is easily manipulated by powerful economic interest groups, as the history of Latin America amply demonstrates. If democratic socialists cannot solve this problem, their program of "correcting" market results in the name of equality will wind up becoming a facade for mercantilism, with all its unequal privileges and monopolies. Weffort's new-model socialists will have given up the old Marxist dream of dramatically transforming labor relations so as to end exploitation. All they will have left will be the cry for more state activism. Let us make no mistake: such activism will mean less power for market forces and more power for state officials and elected politicians. The problem is that there will be no shortage of entrepreneurs, always ready to exploit resources of any kind, who will redirect their energy toward finding ways to manipulate the state sector in their favor. This is the political Achilles' heel of the state interventionism advocated by democratic socialism.

There is another, perhaps deeper, problem. Schumpeter said that "socialism means a new cultural world" and then pointed out how cloudy was the shape of this new world (p. 170). In fact, people who have lived in communist societies do not seem to share specific values different from those of people in capitalist societies. When I visited Russia in 1990, I found that everybody there wanted to shop at Bloomingdale's. Does Sweden embody some new, specifically socialist set of values? Can a new democratic socialism offer a new way of life? And if it cannot, what is the point of a socialism that is unable to change economic institutions to generate a cultural transformation?

The Uncertainty of History

Francis Fukuyama has already laid out his famous theory of the "end of history" in book form.[2] He restricts himself in his present essay to elaborating some of its elements, the chief among these being the nature of the connection between economic development and democracy. I would like to raise two brief objections to his thesis.

Fukuyama presents in his book a variant of the technological theory of history.[3] He asserts that "the progressive and continuous unfolding of modern natural science has provided a directional Mechanism for explaining many aspects of subsequent historical development."[4] I fear, however, that his presentation of this theory has certain drawbacks. Technology is not independent of the legal and economic institutions that can promote or hinder its growth. For example, the development of property rights over discoveries and intellectual goods, along with the existence of a competitive market economy and a tradition of academic freedom to experiment, may do more to determine the expansion of technology than the other way around. Do we need a theory that identifies technology (or any other single cause) as the primary motor of historical change?

Hegel said that the real was rational and the rational was real. As always with Hegel, interpreting his meaning is far from easy, but let us grant for the sake of argument that a free-market system within a liberal democracy is the most rational institutional arrangement available. This arrangement's superior rationality, however, in no way ensures that it will prevail at any given place or time. In history, nothing is inevitable before it happens, and conflicts of race, religion, class, or culture can unleash powerful strains of irrationality and even blind self-destructiveness.

Fukuyama is making not a normative judgment but a prediction when he announces the impending end of history. Hegel, in his *Philosophy of Right*, described the state that he thought would embody freedom and in so doing represent the end of history (history to Hegel being nothing other than the progressive unfolding of freedom). Now according to Hegel, history "ended" in the early nineteenth century. But after that came the rise of Marxism and Nazism, and the "wave of the future" seemed bound to sweep away private property, free contracting, and the other institutions of "rational freedom" à la Hegel. For Alexandre Kojève, history was already over during the years of the Cold War. What then are the practical consequences of the doctrine of the end of history? Where is its empirical relevance? It seems that, even after the end of history, the "universal homogeneous state" is far from inevitable over much of the globe and can be strongly opposed in the name of another ideal. Even in the developed world, is it not at least possible that the ecological movement (which has a certain religious appeal) might one day seriously challenge the predominance of the liberal democratic model? I simply do not see what difference it makes if the theory of the end of history is true or false.

In my view, the ensemble of basic liberal democratic institutions that both Fukuyama and I support could be better conceived in Kantian, rather than Hegelian, terms. Thus the state that embodies freedom should be seen as a transcendental ideal rather than as an empirical result that history predictably produces.

The Chilean Experience

Let me descend now from the heights of Hegel's philosophy to the problem of the relationship between economic development and democracy. The recent history of my own country, Chile, offers some lessons about this relationship. The first lesson, I think, is that a country's prosperity is closely linked to widespread confidence that its elites will make rational decisions. Wealth is in the long run more a matter of institutions than of natural resources or the level of industrialization, for example. Institutions are, among other things, devices designed to make people's behavior more predictable and thereby facilitate rational decision making. Good institutions are *the* best capital that a society can have, and they are precisely what most poor countries lack.

Stable democracy has not always presupposed high levels of economic well-being. Chile and Uruguay are and were significantly poorer than Germany and France, yet throughout the nineteenth century and up until the Second World War, the former pair had a far better democratic record than the latter. The problem now is that modern media of communications have generated desires for rapid growth in living standards. Eventually the disparity between rising expectations and scarce resources brings on populism and its consequences, political and social chaos. Chaos in turn generates cries for order, for the reassertion of authority, for the erection of a coherent and effective decision-making system.

In the case of Chile, this chain of events precipitated the rise of an authoritarian regime. Fear of communism and chaos were behind Chile's military coup in 1973. Its aim was to defeat the former and avoid the latter, not to establish a market economy. Yet after the authoritarian regime restored order, it began channeling economic and social demands into a market system imposed by force. The reasons why the armed forces opted for a free-market economic program are complex, and I have tried to deal with them more fully in another place.[5] Suffice it to say here that the generals were looking for a way to produce the economic stability and growth that they thought were needed to reinforce and legitimize military rule. Then after 17 years, the regime successfully led a transition to democracy. What contribution did capitalism make to the restoration of democratic process?

Conditions of prosperity achieved via capitalism make it more difficult openly to pursue classic socialist policies (though not to vote for socialists). Major transfers of property through nationalization become less likely, for they involve too many politically risky uncertainties. The recent history of post-Franco Spain provides an excellent illustration of this process.

What makes the Chilean case so complex is that, although free-market institutions were established, adverse external circumstances meant that the economic well-being of the population did not rise as fast or as far as planned. Indeed, per capita GNP in 1987 was not much more than per capita GNP in 1970. Nonetheless, the lowering of protective tariffs opened Chile to once-forbidden imports that had come to be viewed as status symbols. Food became more expensive, but used American clothes, refrigerators, television sets, and cars became cheaper. Although one cannot draw any simple connection, in the case of Chile, between rising standards of living and changing political attitudes, consumption patterns and opportunities did change as a result of economic reform. I think that the opening of the economy and the increase in exports helped to rouse feelings of pride, dignity, and hope. To be connected—to be part of the world, and to be able to show it in your clothes and possessions—has a certain value. Furthermore, public welfare programs were improved significantly, and more aid reached the poorest.[6] Still, by the end of the military regime in 1990, public opinion polls showed little support for free-market policies.[7]

However that may be, capitalism did undoubtedly generate more favorable conditions for the exercise of liberties. First, even under authoritarian political rule, there were free spaces in society created by the mere existence of numerous employers, a privately owned media, and the state's decision to limit the scope for political decision making in economic matters. Second, capitalism moved people to aspire to the bourgeois way of life. The elite, but not only the elite, saw opportunities to make money and acquire standing through private enterprise. The rewards offered by the market include a certain type of recognition as well as money. All this made civil society stronger. Third, the workings of capitalism spurred desires for long-run institutional stability which, given Chile's democratic traditions, helped encourage the regime to begin planning the first steps back toward democracy as early as 1980. Finally, the sound condition of the economy by the end of the 1980s made a crucial contribution to the stability of the transition process by allowing the government to operate within a well-defined and smoothly functioning system.

> *"The rewards offered by the market include a certain type of recognition as well as money."*

A summary of Chile's experience since the nineteenth century goes like this: democratic capitalism; democratic mercantilism (urbanization, industrialization, rise of expectations); Marxist-populist revolution; chaos; rising fear of communism and demands for order; authoritarian government; urgent demand for economic growth to stabilize the regime; capitalism; demand for long-run institutional stability; transition to democracy; demand to consolidate democracy; capitalism.

I do not think that capitalism was the most important factor in bringing about Chile's transition to democracy; cultural factors and political developments at the national and international levels seem to me to have been, on the whole, more important.[8] The socialist and Christian Democratic elites' evolving views about political and economic matters, coupled with international developments like the successful democratic transition and consolidation in Spain, were of paramount importance. Once the newly elected government of President Patricio Aylwin made clear its intention to stick with a free-market approach, capitalism began to acquire democratic credentials. This process, which is still going on, was the result of strong leadership. Chile's per capita GNP at the peak of its social, political, and ideological polarization in the early 1970s was very similar to its per capita GNP at the beginning of the new democracy in 1990, when an atmosphere of social peace, consensus, and moderation prevailed. The story of Chile highlights the importance of politics and history and the power of values, ideas, symbols, and social moods. It says little in favor of economic determinism or mechanistic views of history.

Does a poor country in the contemporary world need an authoritarian regime to inaugurate the market system? Although I cannot pretend to know the answer to this question, I will say that in Chile in 1973 it would have been utterly impossible to establish capitalism by democratic means. Argentina today under President Carlos Menem, however, may be charting a democratic path to free markets, although it is still too early to tell. To establish capitalism, you need a strong, consistent, and effective government with a real capacity to lead. For those, like myself, who strongly support free-market reform but are unwilling to countenance the toppling of democracy, the problem is how to bring about the cultural, political, and economic conditions that favor democratic leadership.

NOTES

1. Joseph A. Schumpeter, *Capitalism, Socialism and Democracy*, 3rd ed. (New York: Harper and Row, 1950), 250. All subsequent page references to this work are given in the text above.

2. Francis Fukuyama, *The End of History and the Last Man* (New York: Free Press, 1992).

3. Probably the most interesting philosophy of history of this kind is G.H. Cohen's *Karl Marx's Theory of History* (Princeton: Princeton University Press, 1979).

4. Fukuyama, op. cit., 73.

5. See Arturo Fontaine Talavera, "Sobre el Pecado Original de la Transformación Capitalista," in Barry Levine, ed., *El Desafío Neoliberal* (Bogotá: Grupo Editorial Norma, 1992).

6. Tarsicio Castañeda, *Para Combatir la Pobreza* (Santiago: Centro de Estudios Públicos, 1990).

7. Roberto Méndez, Oscar Godoy, Enrique Barros, and Arturo Fontaine Talavera, "Por qué ganó el 'No'?," *Estudios Públicos* (Santiago) 33 (Summer 1989), 83-134.

8. Ibid., passim.

12.
THE SOCIALIST ALTERNATIVE

Ralph Miliband

Ralph Miliband *is visiting distinguished professor of political science at the Graduate School of the City University of New York. He previously taught at the London School of Economics and Leeds University (England), and was Morris Hillquit Professor of Labor and Social Thought at Brandeis University. His publications include* The State and Capitalist Society *(1969),* Marxism and Politics *(1977), and* Divided Societies *(1989). He is also coeditor of the* Socialist Register, *an annual volume of essays published in London and New York that has appeared regularly since 1964.*

Since Francis Fukuyama's essay takes up some key themes from his book *The End of History and the Last Man*, I think it would be useful for the purposes of this symposium if I were to focus part of my comments on that work itself.[1] The core of Fukuyama's argument is that there is no satisfactory alternative to what he calls liberal democracy (I prefer to call it capitalist democracy). The main challenge to capitalist democracy in this century, he says, was Soviet-style communism, which has now revealed itself to be a definite failure. Other alternatives of one sort or another—fascism, various forms of rightist authoritarianism, or Iranian-style theocracy—remain possible, but they are infinitely less satisfactory than capitalist democracy, and do not in any case correspond to the march of history. The future belongs to capitalist democracy, which represents, in Fukuyama's words, "the end point of mankind's ideological evolution" and the "final form of human government" (p. xi). "Left-wing critics of liberal democracies," he also claims, "are singularly lacking in *radical* solutions to overcoming the more intractable forms of inequality" (p. 293, emphasis in the original).

In opposition to this line of reasoning, I wish to argue that there does indeed exist a radical alternative on the left to capitalist democracy. This alternative is socialist democracy, which has nothing whatsoever to do with Soviet communism, and which Fukuyama altogether fails to consider. He takes note of the many Westerners who hoped that the peoples of the postcommunist countries would use their newly won freedoms to "choose a 'humane' left-wing alternative that was neither communism nor capitalist democracy" (p. 34). This, he quite rightly adds, turned out to be a total illusion. Many socialists who had been bitterly critical of Soviet communism had harbored hopes that the Soviet Union might eventually begin to approximate something that could be called a socialist society. But the illusory nature of these particular hopes tells us nothing about the possibility of socialism.

Fukuyama also notes in an endnote that "in the course of the entire controversy over [my original article on 'The End of History?' in *The National Interest*], no one that I am aware of suggested an alternative form of social organization that he or she personally believed was better" than liberal democracy (pp. 347-48n.10). If so, this proves the present decrepitude of the left, but nothing else. I do want to consider the socialist alternative, which I think is an infinitely more desirable and viable form of social organization than capitalist democracy. In order to prepare the ground for my defense of this view, however, I must first say something about capitalist democracy, and why a radical alternative to it is an essential condition of human progress.

Fukuyama concedes that "liberal democracies are doubtless plagued by a host of problems like unemployment, pollution, drugs, crime, and the like" (p. 288); that the "economic inequality brought about by capitalism *ipso facto* implies unequal recognition" (p. 289); and most remarkably, that "major social inequalities will remain even in the most perfect of liberal societies" (p. 292). This frank admission from so determined an advocate of capitalist democracy is very damaging to his case, not least given his insistence that liberal democracy uniquely satisfies the desire for "recognition" that he locates at the heart of the historical process. Even so, his acknowledgment of the inadequacy of capitalist democracy does not go nearly far enough. There is a much greater and larger indictment to be drawn up against it, of which I can only suggest a few items here.

Let me begin by suggesting that capitalist democracy is a contradiction in terms, for it encapsulates two opposed systems. On the one hand there is capitalism, a system of economic organization that demands the existence of a relatively small class of people who own and control the main means of industrial, commercial, and financial activity, as well as a major part of the means of communication; these people thereby exercise a totally disproportionate amount of influence on politics and society both in their own countries and in lands far beyond their own borders. On the other hand there is democracy, which is based on the *denial* of such preponderance, and which requires a rough *equality of condition* that capitalism, as Fukuyama acknowledges, repudiates by its very nature. Domination and exploitation are ugly words that do not figure in Fukuyama's vocabulary, but they are at the very core of capitalist democracy, and are inextricably linked to it.

One item which is nowadays very little mentioned is that capitalism is a system based on wage labor. Wage labor is work performed for a wage in the service of a private employer who is entitled, by virtue of owning or controlling the means of production, to appropriate and dispose of whatever surplus the workers produce. Employers are constrained by various pressures that limit their freedom to deal with their workers as they will, or to dispose of the surplus they extract. But this merely qualifies their right to extract a surplus and to dispose of it as they think fit. This right is hardly ever questioned and is taken to be "natural," just as slave labor was once thought to be. Wage labor is not slave labor, of course, but it is a social relationship that, from a socialist perspective, is morally abhorrent: no person should work for the private enrichment of another. Communist experience has amply demonstrated that public ownership of the means of production does not by itself do away with exploitation. But exploitation under public ownership is a *deformation*, for a system based on public ownership does not rest on and require exploitation; under conditions of democratic control, it provides the basis for the free and cooperative association of the producers. By contrast, exploitation is the whole purpose of economic activity under private ownership, which makes no sense if it is not to result in the private enrichment (whatever other purpose this may serve) of the owners and controllers of the means of that activity.

The Limits of Capitalist Democracy

There is no question that domination and exploitation are constrained in capitalist democratic regimes, at least in advanced capitalist countries. But this has largely been the result of relentless pressure from below to enlarge political, civic, and social rights in the face of efforts from above to limit and erode such rights.

By the very fact that it is based on a deep and insurmountable class division, capitalist democracy is bound to involve the limitation of democracy so that it may not seriously challenge the power, property, privileges, and position of the people at the top of the social pyramid—more specifically, the holders of corporate power on the one hand and of state power on the other, linked as they are in a difficult but very real partnership. It is thus quite consistent for an ardent admirer of capitalist democracy like Fukuyama to choose what he calls a "strictly formal definition of democracy," and go on to say that "a country is democratic if it grants its people the right to choose their own government through periodic, secret-ballot, multiparty elections, on the basis of universal and equal adult suffrage" (p. 43). But he immediately goes on to add that "it is true that formal democracy alone does not always guarantee equal participation and rights. Democratic procedures can be manipulated by elites, and do not always accurately reflect the will or true self-interests of the people" (p. 43).

The fact is that in capitalist democratic regimes "democratic procedures" *are* manipulated by elites and by the communications media that they control, and *do* serve to pour out a torrent of obfuscations, half-truths, and plain lies. Democratic procedures in such regimes are a simulacrum of democracy, utterly vitiated by the context in which they function. I recently came across a reference to elections in colonial America in which the author notes that the participation in politics which elections involved at the time was "a safety valve, an interlude when the humble could feel a power otherwise denied them, a power that was only half-illusory. And it was also a legitimizing ritual, a rite by which the populace renewed their consent to an oligarchical power structure."[2] This describes perfectly the same process two hundred years later. Incidentally, it is very much the kind of process that Schumpeter, who was not much of a democrat, had in mind when he spoke of democracy. What he meant by it was an "institutional arrangement for arriving at political decisions in which individuals acquire the power to decide by means of a competitive struggle for the people's vote."[3] This is obviously a very narrow definition of democracy, with its focus on competing "teams" of leaders and with popular participation confined mainly to casting a vote. Capitalist democracy is in fact oligarchic rule, tempered by democratic forms.

This is in no way to dismiss the importance of democratic procedures, even under capitalist conditions; it is to point out, rather, that these procedures, under such conditions, are also a means of *containing pressure from below*. That containment is an essential part of class politics from above, in fact its most important part by far.

As I noted earlier, democratic procedures, even under capitalist conditions, do make reform possible. But the very large and unanswered question is whether these procedures make possible a radical challenge to the existing system of power and privilege. We know from experience that a good many such attempts, in various parts of the world, have been cut short by conservative forces who found that democratic procedures had become too dangerous to be allowed to proceed. These conservative forces everywhere in the world have been greatly helped and encouraged by both liberal and conservative leaders in the United States: recall the overthrow of Mohammad Mossadegh in Iran in 1953, of Jacobo Arbenz in Guatemala in 1954, of João Goulart in Brazil in 1964, of Juan Bosch in the Dominican Republic in 1965, of George Papandreou in Greece in 1967, of Salvador Allende in Chile in 1973, and so on—all of them constitutional democratic reformers. This is class politics from above carried out in an international context, and it remains a crucial aspect of the so-called New World Order.

Apologists for capitalism point to its extraordinary productive success, and note that Marx and Engels themselves paid eloquent tribute to it in *The Communist Manifesto* at a time when capitalism was in its childhood. But a crucial item in the indictment of a capitalist social order is precisely that it is unable to make the best use of the immense resources that capitalism has itself created. Despite these immense resources, capitalist societies are marked by appalling poverty and unemployment, inferior collective services, insecurity, illiteracy, and alienation, all of which provide fertile ground for racist, xenophobic, and generally reactionary politics. In other words, capitalism produces a social order in which democracy, even in its shoddy capitalist version, is under permanent threat of erosion.

The Meaning of Socialist Democracy

Now I want to consider the alternative to capitalism that socialist democracy offers. At the outset, it must be emphasized that socialist democracy has nothing to do with the "model," or rather the antimodel, represented by Soviet communism. Socialist democracy involves neither imperative central planning, nor a command economy under bureaucratic state ownership, nor the monopoly of power by the leaders of a single party, nor total control of society by the party and the state, nor the cult of personality. All this has nothing to do with socialism, or for that matter with Marx's Marxism.

Nor does socialism correspond to Schumpeter's definition of it in *Capitalism, Socialism and Democracy.* "By socialist society," he wrote, "we shall designate an institutional pattern in which the control over means of production and over production itself is vested with a central authority—or, as we may say, in which, as a matter of principle, the economic affairs of society belong to the public and not to the private sphere" (p. 167). By defining what he calls "centralist socialism" in this narrow, "economistic" way, Schumpeter is able to make the spurious claim that "a society may be fully and truly socialist and yet be led by an absolute ruler or be organized in the most democratic of all possible ways; it may be aristocratic or proletarian . . . [and so on]" (p. 170).

This conception of socialism runs counter to what it has meant to all shades of socialist thought. However profound have been the disagreements among different schools, there has always been unanimity on the notion that democracy is an intrinsic part of socialism. In fact, socialists have constantly argued not only that socialism without democracy is a gross perversion, but also that democracy is crippled and incomplete without socialism.

What then does socialist democracy mean? It means a "mixed economy," but one in which the relative shares of the public and private sectors under capitalism would be reversed. In a socialist democracy, the main means of economic activity would be under one or another form of public, social, or cooperative ownership, with the greatest possible degree of democratic participation and control. This is not a fashionable notion today, but such a radical extension of the public sphere remains a *sine qua non* for what is after all a cardinal aim of socialism—namely, the dissolution of the existing and profoundly unequal system of power. The market would obviously have an important place in a socialist mixed economy, but it would be paralleled by a certain amount of planning. The capitalist state already engages in some economic planning; a socialist state would do a good deal more, but without aiming at anything like total control of every aspect of the economy.

The danger that all this might in practice come to mean no more than the transfer of power to a bureaucratic state is obvious; this represents one of the main points of tension in the socialist enterprise. In his essay, Francisco Weffort states that "modern democratic society is not a society of the 'minimal state,' but on the contrary presupposes a strong state." This would have to be true of the state in a socialist democracy, but I also agree with Weffort's comment that a democratic society is one in which "civil society and democracy [are] strong enough to control the state." There is no doubt in my mind, however, that there is a genuine point of tension here.

Socialist democracy would embody many of the features of liberal democracy, including the rule of law, the separation of powers, civil liberties, political pluralism, and a vibrant civil society, but it would give them much more effective meaning. It would seek the democratization of the state and of society at all levels. In short, it would give the notion of citizenship a far truer and larger meaning than it could ever have in a class-divided society. Socialist democracy would constitute an *extension* of capitalist democracy, and at the same time a *break* with it.

None of this could be achieved at a stroke. The realization of socialist democracy is a process that would stretch over many decades and could even be said to be never-ending. Unlike Fukuyama's view in relation to liberal democracy, I do not see socialist democracy as "the end of history." It will harbor many contradictions and involve constant struggle against all the obstacles that stand in the way of ever greater democracy.

Socialist democracy seems to me to offer an immeasurably more desirable goal than capitalist democracy. Yet I would argue that there is nothing remotely "utopian" about it. There can be no illusion about the difficulties that stand in the way of achieving socialist democracy, but neither is there any good reason to think that these difficulties cannot be overcome.

Of course, the prospects for its advancement, let alone its realization, do not appear very good at the moment. There is at present no large constituency anywhere for the kind of changes that socialist democracy implies; insofar as it has to rely on majority support, it has a long way to go. It should be kept in mind, however, that popular majorities for radical change *have* been found again and again in liberal democracies, even if most of the voters were not socialists. As long as capitalism, with all its inherent faults, endures, so long will the socialist alternative remain alive; indeed, it will gain more and more ground as capitalism shows itself to be incapable of solving the major problems confronting humankind. For this reason, the collapse of communism, far from delivering a fatal blow to the socialist alternative, will increasingly be seen as wholly irrelevant to its prospects.

NOTES

1. Francis Fukuyama, *The End of History and the Last Man* (New York: Free Press, 1992). All subsequent page references to this work appear in the text above.

2. Edmund S. Morgan, *Inventing the People: The Rise of Popular Sovereignty in England and America* (London and New York: W.W. Norton, 1988), 206.

3. Joseph A. Schumpeter, *Capitalism, Socialism and Democracy*, 3rd ed. (New York: Harper and Row, 1950), 269. All subsequent page references to this work appear in the text above.

13.
CONCLUDING REFLECTIONS

Seymour Martin Lipset

Seymour Martin Lipset, who formerly taught at Harvard and Stanford universities, is currently Hazel Professor of Public Policy at George Mason University in Fairfax, Virginia, and Senior Fellow at the Hoover Institution. The only social scientist ever to have been elected as president of both the American Sociological Association and the American Political Science Association, he is the author or coauthor of 21 books and the editor or coeditor of 25 more. Among his most well-known publications are Union Democracy *(with Martin Trow and James Coleman, 1956),* Political Man *(1960),* The First New Nation *(1963), and* Continental Divide *(1990).*

How well does Joseph A. Schumpeter's *Capitalism, Socialism and Democracy* stand up after 50 years?[1] The appearance of this volume marking the fiftieth anniversary of its publication attests to the work's continuing importance. A dozen scholars from nine different countries have evaluated the book and come up with disparate conclusions.

The climate in which these recent essays appear is, of course, quite different from the one to which Joseph Schumpeter was reacting. He was writing in the late 1930s and early 1940s—years that saw worldwide economic depression, the rise of fascism, and the outbreak of global war. Western democracy and capitalism were in trouble. Democracy was going downhill, not up. Various forms of right-wing authoritarianism had taken over Italy, Germany, Austria, Spain, Greece, and most of Eastern Europe and Latin America. Capitalism seemed an ineffective system, with the Great Depression persisting in North America and Europe right up until the onset of World War II. Center-left efforts to end the downturn with Keynesian pump-priming failed in France under Premier Léon Blum and in the United States under President Franklin Delano Roosevelt.

These conditions did not lead Schumpeter to reject capitalism. Despite the emergence of large oligopolistic structures that sought to stabilize markets through monopolistic practices, he continued to maintain that capitalism was better at producing material progress, increased productivity, and higher standards of living than any other conceivable system, including all varieties of socialism. For capitalism is inherently evolving: "The fundamental impulse that sets and keeps the capitalist engine in motion comes from the new consumers' goods, the new methods of production or transportation, the new markets, the new forms of industrial organization that capitalist enterprise creates" (p. 83). The system is characterized by "creative destruction," by a kind of chaos that humbles once dominant nations or firms if they fail to respond quickly to innovations or economic crisis. Schumpeter would have seen the decline of IBM and General Motors, or the rise of Japanese companies, as examples of how creative destruction works to produce better products.

Surprisingly, given this emphasis, one finds the classical liberal Schumpeter answering the question "Can capitalism survive?" with a resounding "No." Unlike some other famous prophets of capitalism's doom, however, Schumpeter was not a socialist but a pessimist. As he put it: "Prognosis does not imply anything about the desirability of the course of events one predicts. . . . One may hate socialism . . . and yet foresee its advent" (p. 61).

Capitalism would fall, he explained, because it inevitably "produced . . . [an] atmosphere of almost universal hostility to its own social order" (p. 143). He argued first that "the very success of capitalist enterprise paradoxically tends to impair the prestige or social weight of the class primarily associated with it [i.e., the entrepreneurial bourgeoisie] and that the giant unit of control [the large corporation] tends to oust the bourgeoisie from the functions to which it owed that social weight" (p. 139). The decline of family-owned businesses "takes the life out of the idea of property. . . . Dematerialized, defunctionalized and absentee ownership does not . . . call forth moral allegiance as the vital form of property did" (p. 142). Hence capitalism loses much of its moral legitimacy, and an anticapitalist social atmosphere emerges.

Capitalism and the Intellectuals

Second, and in Schumpeter's judgment even more important, was the "emergence of active hostility" rooted in an alienated class (p. 145). Marx, of course, found this class in the proletariat. Schumpeter, too, recognized the anticapitalist role of the workers, but believed that the intelligentsia posed an even more formidable problem. He defined members of this class as "people who wield the power of the spoken and the written word." Intellectuals are characterized by a "critical attitude" toward institutions (p. 147). They are inherently suspicious of the established, since their occupational role requires them to be innovative;

they are rewarded for originality, which as Thorstein Veblen once pointed out, involves the rejection of the previously accepted. Perhaps anticipating recent developments in the ranks of the Modern Language Association, Schumpeter even noted that "from the criticism of a text to the criticism of a society, the way is shorter than it seems" (p. 148).

The intellectuals' hostility to capitalism ironically "increases, instead of diminishing, with every achievement of capitalist evolution" (p. 153). For capitalism, as it develops, reveals itself more and more as an "unromantic and unheroic civilization" that reflects the tastes and preferences of that prosaic creature, *homo economicus* (p. 160). The capitalist system, therefore, "stands its trial before judges who have the sentence of death in their pockets," whose motives are "extrarational" (p. 144). They are attracted to a utopian emotionalism that "aims at higher goals than full bellies. . . . First and foremost, socialism means a new cultural world . . . hence no merely economic argument for or against can ever be decisive" (p. 170).

The capitalist order, therefore, cannot "control its intellectual sector effectively" (p. 151). Over time, and with the aid of labor movements, the intellectuals will undermine capitalism's legitimacy by "nibbling" it to death. The "intellectual group cannot help nibbling, because it lives on criticism and its whole position depends on criticism that stings; and criticism of persons and of current events will, in a situation in which nothing is sacrosanct, fatally issue in criticism of classes and institutions" (p. 151). Ironically, anticapitalist ideology and critiques of the market system today remain strongest in the heartland of twentieth-century capitalism, the United States. American intellectuals have fostered what the literary critic Lionel Trilling once called the "adversary culture," which tends as a matter of course to look askance at bourgeois and national-patriotic values. Intellectuals have long been the strongest supporters of the relatively small far-left tendencies in American politics, including the various radical third parties that have sprung up from time to time in the country's history.

The judgment that Marxism is alive and relatively well in American intellectualdom is prevalent. As Garry Abrams notes, "American universities may be one of the last bastions of intellectual Marxism, at least in the developed world."[2] Oxford political theorist John Gray also concludes that "the academic institutions of capitalist America will be the last redoubt of Marxist theorizing."[3] Writing in the *New York Review of Books* on the attitudes and writings of American elite scientists, Cambridge University Nobel laureate M.F. Perutz notes that "Marxism may be discredited in Eastern Europe, but it still seems to flourish at Harvard."[4] Commenting in a similar way on the differences between American and Soviet academic literary criticism, Robert Alter points out that "Literature in our own academic circles is regularly dismissed, castigated as an instrument of ideologies of oppression."[5] The ideological left is also strong in Hollywood and among creative personnel in television.

In recent years, this pattern has also been prevalent abroad, where intellectuals and students form most of the support for ecological movements and the "green" political parties associated with them. Nonetheless, the bulk of the intelligentsia in Europe and Japan has now dropped its former allegiance to Marxism. This change stems in part from intellectuals' past links to strong socialist, labor, and (in Italy and France) communist parties. Utopian socialism, in both its authoritarian and democratic forms, has clearly failed. Many intellectuals previously involved with socialist politics have turned away from it, although they continue to nibble at the foundations of capitalism.

Requirements for Democracy

Schumpeter's pessimism about the future of capitalism compelled him to fear for the prospects of democracy as well, for he held that "modern democracy is a product of the capitalist process." He left open, however, the question as to "whether or not democracy is one of those products of capitalism which are to die out with it." The interests of the bourgeoisie lead it to seek to limit "the sphere of public authority"; it follows that it "is easier for a class whose interests are best served by being left alone to practice democratic self-restraint than it is for classes that naturally try to live on the state" (pp. 297-98).

Writing during the heyday of fascism (a movement that he did not discuss directly), Schumpeter concluded that the facts seemed to suggest "a pessimistic prognosis" for bourgeois democracy. The most important reason for this, he thought, lay not merely in the projected spread of socialist systems, but also in the inherent increase in conflict in industrial societies, for "the democratic method never works at its best when nations are much divided on fundamental questions of social structure" (p. 298).

Believing that socialism rather than fascism would win out, Schumpeter was concerned about the prospects for democracy under the former. Given his emphasis on the delimitation of politics as a condition for a free society, it is understandable that he warns: "No responsible person can view with equanimity the consequences of extending the democratic method, that is to say the sphere of 'politics,' to all economic affairs" (p. 299). He stresses the dangers inherent in socialist society's lack of

the automatic restrictions imposed upon the political sphere by the bourgeois scheme of things. Moreover, in socialist society it will no longer be possible to find comfort in the thought that the inefficiencies of political procedure are after all a guarantee of freedom. Lack of efficient management will spell lack of bread. (p. 299)

Yet as we have noted, Schumpeter did not believe that the victory of socialism would lead inevitably to the end of democracy. "Operating socialist democracy," he said, "would be a perfectly hopeless task except in the case of a society that fulfills all the requirements of [democratic] 'maturity.'" These requirements could be met only in a highly stable, solidly institutionalized democracy, where socialists rose to power through elections, and where "the vast majority of the people in all classes are resolved to abide by the rules of the democratic game," which "in turn implies that they are substantially agreed on the fundamentals of their institutional structure" (p. 301). Such conditions have been elaborated by Robert Dahl in his classic work, *Polyarchy.*[6] These, of course, include regular free elections with full suffrage and a secret ballot, as well as turnover among responsible officeholders. They presumably can be met only in economically developed and stable polities, such as are found in Western Europe and North America.

The basic problem of democracy is the need to institutionalize peaceful struggle among competing elites that offer the masses the opportunity to choose between alternative programs even as they expose one another's weaknesses and failings. Thus a basic condition for a stable democracy is institutionalized parties embedded in a functioning civil society: "They constitute an attempt to regulate political competition exactly similar to the corresponding practices of a trade association. The psycho-technics of party management and party advertising, slogans and marching tunes, are not accessories. They are of the essence of politics" (p. 283).

Totalitarian systems sought systematically to eliminate groups mediating between the individual and the state, and so have left their successors without effective civil societies. This reduced the possibility for *organized* opposition by reducing group effectiveness generally, leaving individuals ill-suited for innovative activities like entrepreneurship or anything else that Tocqueville included under the heading of "civil partnerships." The countries of the former Soviet empire are now trying to cope with the consequences of the suppression of civil society, which makes it hard to consolidate democracy or foster economic entrepreneurship. Fortunately, most of the younger democracies outside the ex-communist bloc, such as Spain and Chile, never experienced totalitarianism and hence retained some of the pluralist institutions of civil society even while under autocratic rule.

Political Parties and Electoral Systems

Political parties themselves should be viewed as mediating institutions between the citizenry and the state. A crucial condition for a stable democracy is the presence of major parties with large and virtually permanent bases of support among voters. That support should be so uncritical as to survive clear-cut policy failures and scandals. If such loyalty exists, parties can never be totally wiped out and can always supply a basis for effective opposition. The Republican Party in the Depression-era United States, for example, though declining sharply in electoral support, remained a major opposition party despite the hard times that began on its watch. A similar process of delegitimization in the wake of the early-1970s Watergate scandal did not prevent a Republican comeback in the 1980s.

In new political systems, in which parties do not command firm allegiance, some can be easily eliminated. The Hamiltonian Federalist Party, which competed in the early years of the American Republic with the Jeffersonian Democratic-Republicans, declined sharply after losing the presidency in 1800 and was soon extinct. In more recent postauthoritarian European polities, early democratic movements that appeared to have mass support—such as the Party of Action in postwar Italy and the Union of the Democratic Center in Spain (which in 1977 formed a majority government after the first post-Franco elections), the Civic Forum in Czechoslovakia, or Solidarity in Poland—all suffered extinction or near-extinction in early elections. The pattern has repeated itself in a number of newly independent republics of the former Soviet Union. It might even be argued that the presence of at least two parties with a loyal mass base comes close to being a necessary condition for stable democracy. Without strong parties, democracy is unlikely to survive.

Procedures for choosing and changing governments are also among the principal factors affecting the prospects for democratic stability. Elections that offer voters an effective way to throw incumbents out will provide more stability and legitimacy than can be had in systems where electoral rules or the general balance of political forces makes change difficult.

Electoral systems like those found in the United States and much of the British Commonwealth feature single-member districts that press the public to choose between two major parties. Voters know that if they turn against the government party, they can replace it with the opposition. Parties in such systems tend to be heterogeneous coalitions, and many voters frequently opt for the "lesser evil." Moreover, since the opposition usually promises to reverse course, incumbents can be punished for unpopular policies or for presiding over depressing events. Where pure proportional representation (PR) and its concomitant multiple parties have existed, whether in Weimar Germany, pre-Fascist Italy, much of Eastern Europe after the First World War, or present-day Israel, the electorate often has little say in the actual composition of the government. Where no party has a majority, changing coalitions must be formed out of diverse forces. A party in the governing coalition may increase its votes, only to find itself excluded from the new cabinet that is formed after the election. Small, opportunistic, or special-interest parties may hold the balance of power, and thus determine the shape and policies of postelection coalitions. New parties can spring up overnight.

Such systems can be improved. Attributing the instability of the Third and Fourth French republics to multiparty parliamentary systems that produced many short-lived and ineffectual cabinets, Charles de Gaulle was able in 1958 to introduce a complex system featuring a powerful president who shared power with a premier and cabinet of ministers. The change has seemingly led to more focused contests between the left and the right, and to more effective and longer-lived governments.

Under socialism, as Schumpeter correctly argued, democracy can only work where no great sacrifices need be required of one generation for the benefit of a later one. "But even if there is no necessity for sweating the people by means of a Gosplan, the task of keeping the democratic course may prove to be extremely delicate. . . . After all, effective management of the socialist economy means dictatorship not *of* but *over* the proletariat in the factory" (p. 302). Defining socialism as "an institutional pattern in which the control over means of production and over production itself is vested with a central authority—or, as we may say, in which, as a matter of principle, the economic affairs of society belong to the public and not to the private sphere" (p. 167), Schumpeter concluded that "there is little reason to believe that [it] will mean the advent of the civilization of which orthodox socialists dream. It is much more likely to present fascist features" (p. 375).

Reevaluating Schumpeter's Analysis

Fifty years after Schumpeter made those pessimistic remarks, we seek to evaluate them in our own very different era. The record shows that Schumpeter was right about the difficulties of making socialism work as an economic system, particularly in less developed, primarily agrarian societies. Three-quarters of a century after the Russian Revolution, communism has collapsed in Eastern Europe and the ex-Soviet Union, and is seeking to transform itself into a predominantly market economy in China and Vietnam. We now know that it was an enormous failure economically, that conditions in the former Soviet Union were much worse than even its most severe critics imagined or tried to document. In effect, the former Soviet republics (including Russia) are Third World nations.

History, however, has proved Schumpeter wrong about the political failure of capitalism, which is more broadly accepted over larger sections of the world than ever before. And all the social democratic parties from Sweden to Italy, from Chile to Israel, have explicitly acknowledged the superiority of market economies to planned economies. As Spanish Socialist premier Felipe González has noted (in a formulation that resembles Churchill's comments on democracy), competitive free-market economies may be marred by greed, corruption, and exploitation of the weak, but "capitalism is the least bad economic system in existence."

"Democracy is ascendant as never before in history.... For the first time, the majority of the member states of the United Nations may be considered free societies."

Few leftist parties today still advocate socialism, and those that do tend to be small and marginalized.[7]

Democracy is ascendant as never before in history. Beginning with the political openings in Greece, Portugal, and Spain in the mid-1970s, authoritarian regimes have been transformed into more or less competitive multiparty systems across almost all of Latin America, in parts of East Asia and Africa, and in most of the formerly communist countries of Eastern Europe and what was once called the Soviet Union. Over four dozen polities have been so changed since the mid-1970s. For the first time, the majority of the member states of the United Nations may be considered free societies. The one group of nations to resist the democratic trend has been the predominantly Muslim ones.

In seeking to evaluate Schumpeter, the authors who contributed to this volume considered the question whether the return to or emergence of capitalism in the countries of Eastern Europe and the former Soviet Union will help to produce stable democracies.[8] Not surprisingly, Francis Fukuyama is the most optimistic. But even his anticipation is qualified. As he notes:

> The relationship between capitalism and democracy is an indirect one. That is, capitalism in itself does not generate direct pressures for democracy. It is perfectly compatible with many forms of authoritarianism (though obviously not with communist totalitarianism), and may even flourish better in nondemocracies. But capitalism is a more efficient engine of economic growth than socialism, and thus is more likely to generate the rapid socioeconomic change that favors the emergence of stable democracy.[9]

Hungarian philosopher G.M. Tamás, a leader of the classical-liberal grouping within the Free Democratic Alliance, is the most pessimistic of our analysts. He argues that cultural conditions in Eastern and Central Europe have been and remain fundamentally different from those which gave rise to capitalism and democracy in the West. Modernity did not develop in the East, whose traditions remain "strongly anti-individualistic." The anticommunist nationalist right in Eastern Europe "hates capitalism."

The revolution in most of these countries is populist, majoritarian, and antipluralist. "There is nothing about it that is [classically] liberal":

All the surveys and polling data show that public opinion in our region rejects dictatorship, but would like to see a strong man at the helm; favors popular government, but hates parliament, parties, and the press; likes social welfare legislation and equality, but not trade unions; wants to topple the present government, but disapproves of the idea of a regular opposition; supports the notion of the market (which is a code word for Western-style living standards), but wishes to punish and expropriate the rich and condemns banking for preying on simple working people; favors a guaranteed minimum income, but sees unemployment as an immoral state and wants to punish or possibly deport the unemployed.[10]

Recent history bears Tamás out. In Lithuania, the first Soviet republic to secede from the Soviet Union and abandon communism, the reformed communist party won the November 1992 elections with a majority vote, while those who led the break have been left on the sidelines. In Poland, the old official unions are now larger than Solidarity, and the Alliance of the Democratic Left—actually the Communists under a new name—holds one of the largest blocs of seats in parliament. The anticommunist independent unions are much weaker than the old official ones everywhere in the successor states of the former Soviet Union, and these old unions successfully slow down or stop efforts at privatization. Networks of "former" communists continue to dominate governments and economies. At the same time, declines in productivity, food supplies, employment, and law and order are blamed on neoliberals, even though the latter have never really wielded power.

As Peter Berger and Jagdish Bhagwati emphasize in their respective essays, Western and liberal triumphalism is "premature" and "unwarranted," but so is Adam Przeworski's concern over the dysfunctions of as yet largely nonexistent neoliberal markets in Eastern Europe and the ex-Soviet Union, which he believes are not conducive to economic growth or strong representative institutions.[11] Statism still dominates economic life in all of these countries.

Berger, who is the most realistic of the authors, notes that it is "far from certain that the [capitalist] transition will even occur in all these societies, under democratic or any other auspices. . . . The entire shift to capitalism may . . . find itself stopped dead, while political rulers reimpose some variety of 'emergency socialism' that might well become permanently institutionalized."[12] The system need not be called socialist—populism or nationalism will serve as a better rubric for purposes of public relations.

South Korea's Kyung-won Kim, however, directs attention to the successful record of economic development under state and nondemocratic auspices in the noncommunist world, especially Japan and Germany. Relying on the researches of Ralf Dahrendorf, he reports:

The German case shows that when capitalist industrialization is initiated and guided by the state instead of by a politically autonomous bourgeoisie, an authoritarian regime can preempt the rise of liberal democracy by coopting or diverting those groups that would otherwise press for democracy.[13]

Programs of authoritarian *dirigisme*, which seek to spur development by using market mechanisms as tools to motivate behavior and allocate resources, have been tried in both noncommunist countries (such as South Korea and Taiwan) and communist ones (like China and Vietnam). These inevitably produce a state of affairs that Kim (following Robert Scalapino) calls "authoritarian pluralism." By doing so, "the authoritarian-pluralist regime is either wittingly or unwittingly making possible the emergence of a middle class." And this class will inevitably "begin making political claims against the authoritarian regime."[14] The East European and Asian experiences offer a kind of test of Schumpeterian analysis. In the former, democratic reforms continue to rest on a socialist economic base, which resists transformation. In the latter, capitalism emerges and grows, while the authoritarian single-party regimes continue to hold power. But as Kim notes, following Schumpeter: "It is in the nature of capitalism that it secretly nurtures and eventually unleashes democratic forces." Hence we may anticipate the manifestation in Asia of "democratic forces unleashed by an assertive middle class that the state itself has indirectly fostered."[15] As Bhagwati asserts, Deng Xiaoping's emphasis on economic development in China may yet lead to freedom for that country, while Gorbachev's efforts in the old USSR failed decisively.

In the ex-Soviet Union, socialism is being refurbished under other names, sustained by the *nomenklatura*, by the still very potent ex-communist trade unions (which retain control of welfare and housing functions), and by a complex of "traditional" groups that prefer state control over the economy. Unless these institutions are weakened through the emergence of a new bourgeois class, privatization, and the creation of genuinely independent trade unions, the continued state "monopoly of the economic sphere leaves little or . . . no space within official public life for criticism or opposition."[16]

History in Fukuyama's neo-Hegelian sense is not dead, for statist socialism is alive, even if Marxism and communism no longer survive as legitimating ideologies. Fukuyama's premise (and that of much other Western writing) is that socialism as practiced in the former Marxist-Leninist states is finished. Happily, it is indeed a spent force in eastern Germany, Hungary, Poland, and the Czech Republic, but this is not yet the case elsewhere. There is a determined ex-communist ruling class entrenched within still powerful statist economic institutions in the former Soviet Union and much of Eastern Europe. The desire of the old ruling class to retain its privileges, combined with the desire of so many workers, peasants, minor bureaucrats, and military officers for economic security and sociopolitical stability, points toward the possibility of a Restoration. It is sobering to recall how few revolutions, aside from the American, have ever succeeded.

Continuing Challenges to Capitalism

The sweeping shift to ideological approval of capitalism and the free market, while seemingly universal, may nonetheless prove to be of short duration. Even friends of these institutions, such as Schumpeter and, more recently, Irving Kristol, have noted that democratic capitalism, unlike socialism and communism, makes no pretense of being able definitively to solve major human problems. Even in purely economic terms, the free market offers no cure-all and promises no utopia. At best, it holds out the promise of an unrigged lottery, but as in all such contests, the jackpots go to a minority of players. Hence there must be many who are (at least in a relative sense) "losers"; some of these will be receptive to reformist or anticapitalist movements. The capitalist distribution of rewards must be greatly unequal, and as Tocqueville pointed out a century and a half ago, the idea of equality impels the underprivileged to support redistributionist parties and policies.

At the center of free market ideology is an emphasis on self-interest, or to put it in invidious terms, on greed. From Adam Smith to Milton Friedman, the argument has been made that the uninhibited pursuit of personal or institutional gain will result in a steadily growing economy from which all benefit regardless of status or wealth. As we know, however, not only are there individual variations in achievement, but also substantial differences among countries in economic performance. Moreover, the business cycle, a fixture of market economies, not only fosters growth but implies downswings—periods of increased unemployment, high inflation, or perhaps even both.

Renewed disdain for capitalism is also predictable because of the tendency of market-based societies to stress cool and mundane rationality at the expense of burning idealism. As Kristol argues:

> [T]he real trouble [with capitalism] is not sociological or economical at all. It is that the "middling" nature of a bourgeois society falls short of corresponding adequately to the full range of man's spiritual nature, which makes more than middling demands upon the universe, and demands more than middling answers. This weakness of bourgeois society has been highlighted by intellectual critics from the very beginning.[17]

Capitalism fails to generate effective community values. Its failures have placed it at odds with many religious communities. The Roman Catholic Church offers a current example as it makes the case for a more solidaristic, even familial, model of social relations. The present pope,

John Paul II, played a major role in the fall of communism in his native Poland and stands firmly in the papal tradition of opposition to socialism, but he is also an incisive critic of capitalism. He has warned repeatedly of the inherent dangers of selfishness, inequality, and poverty in capitalist societies. His dim view of unfettered markets places him in accord with a longstanding Catholic penchant for communitarian notions of *noblesse oblige* and certain forms of social welfarism.

> "The struggle between the left, understood as the party of greater equality, and the right, understood as the defender of the status quo, is not over."

Capitalism does not promise to fulfill profound spiritual longings or to eliminate inequality, poverty, racism, sexism, pollution, and war; small wonder that it cannot appeal in idealistic terms to the young. And as Aristotle emphasized 2500 years ago, the young—and it may be added, intellectuals—look for total solutions. Hence new movements and new ideologies—even old ones that hold out reformist and utopian promises—will appear or reappear on the world scene. Communitarian concerns will relegitimate the state as a tool for reducing if not eliminating inequalities of race, gender, and social status. To these may be added environmental concerns. Not surprisingly, such issues have begun to take priority among both older and newer parties on the left. Classical liberals will resist the policy agendas of social democrats and Greens alike on the grounds that both require too much interference with the market and free competition.

Francisco Weffort even sees socialism as politically viable if it focuses on noneconomic values. He argues:

> [S]ocialists can feel as confident as ever about old socialist values like equality, social justice, and so on. It is this "cultural" dimension of socialism that explains why there are still so many socialists in the world. . . . Thus it will not be surprising if socialists, given their lack of alternative economic and social theories, embrace in the coming years a conception of socialism that is not bound up with a particular system but is defined primarily in terms of values.[18]

The struggle between the left, understood as the party of greater equality, and the right, understood as the defender of the status quo, is not over. In ex-communist countries, the terms "left-wing" and "liberal" are now used to describe advocates of the free market and democracy who seek to reduce the power of state bureaucracies, while the words "right-wing" and "conservative" refer to groups that defend state controls. Ironically, this is the way that these ideological concepts were originally used throughout much of the nineteenth century. Following the rise of socialist movements, however, "leftist" came to mean favoring greater emphasis on community and equality, with the state as the primary instrument of reform. The right, linked to establishments on the defensive, has been identified, particularly since World War II, with opposition to governmental intervention. Even if socialism is now a dirty word, the contest between these two orientations is by no means over. Profound political conflict—which is to say, history—will surely continue.

NOTES

1. Joseph A. Schumpeter, *Capitalism, Socialism and Democracy*, 3rd ed. (New York: Harper and Row, 1950). For all citations of this work, page numbers will appear in the text.

2. Garry Abrams, "After the Wall: As New Era Emerges U.S. Political Thinkers Ponder Fate of Marxism," *Los Angeles Times*, 6 December 1989, E2, E6.

3. John Gray, "Fashion, Fantasy, or Fiasco," *Times Literary Supplement*, 24 February-2 March 1989, 183.

4. M.F. Perutz, "High on Science," *New York Review of Books*, 16 August 1990, 15.

5. Robert Alter, "Tyrants and Butterflies," *New Republic*, 15 October 1990, 43.

6. Robert A. Dahl, *Polyarchy: Participation and Opposition* (New Haven: Yale University Press, 1971).

7. For detailed documentation and analysis of the changes in social democratic parties, see Seymour Martin Lipset, "No Third Way: A Comparative Perspective on the Left," in Daniel Chirot, ed., *The Crisis of Leninism and the Decline of the Left: The Revolutions of 1989* (Seattle: University of Washington Press, 1991), 183-232.

8. For a review of the literature on capitalism and democracy, see Gabriel Almond, "Capitalism and Democracy," *PS: Political Science* 24 (September 1991): 467-74.

9. See above, p. 102.

10. See above, p. 67.

11. The comments by Berger and Bhagwati may be found on pp. 2 and 35 above.

12. See above, p. 9.

13. See above, p. 19.

14. See above, pp. 21-22.

15. See above, p. 23.

16. See above, p. 23.

17. Irving Kristol, *Two Cheers for Capitalism* (New York: Basic Books, 1978), esp. 153-87, 255-70.

18. See above, p. 90.

INDEX OF PROPER NAMES